H.O.L.

12

–The Guardian Guide to the Economy

VOLUME 2

The Guardian Guide to the Economy

VOLUME 2

**FRANCES CAIRNCROSS
AND PHIL KEELEY**

METHUEN

First published in 1983 by
Methuen & Co. Ltd
11 New Fetter Lane, London EC4P 4EE

Typeset by Scarborough Typesetting Services
and printed in Great Britain by
Richard Clay (The Chaucer Press) Ltd
Bungay, Suffolk

British Library Cataloguing in Publication Data

Cairncross, Frances
The Guardian guide to the economy.
Vol. 2
1. Great Britain − Economic conditions − 1945−
I. Title   II. Keeley, Phil
330.941′0858   HC256.6

ISBN 0−416−35310−X
ISBN 0−423−51150−5

Contents

Preface

Any mug can extrapolate: but guessing where a trend will turn is one of the most difficult things in economics. It was this which made the second *Guardian Guide to the Economy* a more difficult book to write than the first. For as we went to press, in the late spring of 1983, it looked very much as though the British economy might be beginning to stage some sort of recovery — and just possible that the world economy would be stimulated by the sharp fall in the oil price into a revival. But the upturn was likely to be weak by post-war standards.

It is possible that some of the gloom which pervades some of the chapters will be overtaken by an upturn. But in economics, it usually pays to be a pessimist. The profound recession of the early 1980s has left a disturbing legacy of Third World debt (the subject of chapter 5) and mounting protectionism (the subject of chapter 4) which will make that debt difficult to repay. And even if the recession retreats, it looks as if it has overlaid and accentuated problems which were already building up in the 1970s and even the late 1960s. These problems were revealed in structural changes in the labour market (discussed in chapter 3), a decline in manufacturing employment in several industrial countries which may be related to the new industrialization of some countries of the Third World.

Even if the recession passes, the old industrialized countries will still have to learn to live with these new competitors. Britain is not obviously well placed to do so. The Conservative experiment with monetary policy (the subject of chapter 1) has resulted in a striking decline in inflation, but it is not at all clear that there has been any fundamental change in the way pay is determined (the theme of chapter 2) or in the balance between the public and private sectors (one of the issues in chapter 6).

If this book is not jolly reading, it ought at least to be comprehensible. It is intended, like its predecessor, to illuminate the issues behind the economic stories in the quality newspapers: to give a starting point for anyone who is interested in issues such as exchange rate policy or incomes policy, but who has not really gained a foothold in the debate. It is also, of course, aimed at sixth-form students: which is why it includes exercises (of inscrutable complication for anyone not doing A-levels). The suggestions for further reading are meant as a short guide to the sort of literature journalists use to keep tabs on the economy, and as a source of ideas for free material for schoolteachers — not as a comprehensive bibliography.

Several people helped to catch howlers and disentangle woolly thinking in earlier drafts. They include Peter Rodgers, John Carvel and John Torode of the *Guardian*; Alan Budd; Alec Cairncross; and Hamish McRae, who provided hot meals, child minding and sensible comments on Third World debt.

Frances Cairncross

* * *

The aim of the question material in this book is to show that the issues developed in the articles can be explored using simple, some might mistakenly say elementary, models.

In the study of economics people often do not realize that the simplest of models can provide the most powerful of insights. It is all too easy to finish a course knowing a great deal of economics but understanding little of economic controversy. This recognition has enhanced my personal enjoyment of the subject and I am indebted to David Gowland at the University of York for this. My thanks also to the students of Henbury School, Bristol for their stubborn refusal to be impressed by complexity of argument unless it yielded understanding of current issues.

Phil Keeley

1 Monetary policy – how well has it worked?

'A very interesting laboratory experiment for economics' is how the distinguished American professor, James Tobin, described the policies of Mrs Thatcher's government when he appeared before the House of Commons Treasury Committee in 1981. Two years later, most mainstream economists in Britain would have argued that the experiment had been a disastrous failure. The attempt to make monetary policy the principal instrument of economic management had indeed led to a dramatic fall in the rate of inflation. But the cost had been a staggering rise in unemployment and fall in output.

The supporters of the strategy, both inside and outside the government, were still claiming that the experiment was not yet complete. It would not be possible to be sure of the value of monetary policy, they insisted, until economic recovery began. This chapter examines the evidence so far: the extent to which there has been a retreat from the original policy, and the extent to which monetary policy may be held responsible for such success as the Thatcher government appears to have had.

The first point to realize is that monetary targets were not the invention of the Conservative government when it took office in May 1979. In the Letter of Intent to the International Monetary Fund in December 1976, the Labour government had set out a forecast for monetary growth. In the 1977 Budget, that forecast became more prescriptive, and a year later the Chancellor of the Exchequer, Mr Healey, introduced the concept of rolling targets for monetary growth six months ahead.

Nor was it new for a government to tell voters that it was not possible to 'spend one's way out of trouble'. The toughest and most categorical statement of this view is in a speech made by James Callaghan when he was Prime Minister to the Labour Party conference at Blackpool in 1976.

What was new about the Conservative government's approach was the overriding importance it attached to reducing inflation, and its confident belief that monetary policy offered the key to success. This led it to set monetary targets not merely for six months ahead but — in the March 1980 Budget — a four-year programme of diminishing monetary growth. This was to be underwritten by a decline in the Public Sector Borrowing Requirement, which was regarded as the most controllable influence on monetary growth, [1]* and in the size of the government's deficit relative to Gross Domestic Product. This innovation was called the Medium Term Financial Strategy (MTFS in the jargon), and the government regarded it as the absolute keystone of its economic policies. The reason for expounding it, at least initially, was the belief that if people could be brought to expect inflation to slow down, they would adjust their behaviour accordingly. [2, 3] Workers would ask for smaller pay rises, lenders would accept lower interest rates, and businesses would become more confident.

As time went by, and the influence of the MTFS on inflationary expectations proved hard to trace, it acquired another justification. It provided a framework for government policy, rather as the fixed exchange rate had done in the period up to 1971, and offered proof of what some would see as the government's blind inflexibility: others, as its strong-minded refusal to be influenced by short-term changes in output.

For a further central plank of the government's belief was that it was simply not possible for it to raise the level of output or to reduce unemployment in anything but the short term. Earlier governments had believed (to caricature a bit) that they controlled unemployment and the trade unions controlled the rate of inflation. Mrs Thatcher's supporters would have argued precisely the reverse. The pace of inflation, in anything but the short term, was controlled by the government by way of the money supply. Through its control over the level of public spending, the government had in its hands what it believed was one of the main determinants of monetary growth: the amount of government borrowing. On the other hand, unemployment was under the control of the trade

* The numbers in brackets refer to the questions at the end of each chapter.

2

unions. If they jacked up wages, and the government did not respond by allowing the money supply to rise, there would simply be fewer jobs to go round. So the Trades Union Congress found itself deprived of the ritual of beer and sandwiches at midnight at Number 10, which had been so important a part of the anti-inflation policies of previous governments, and treated instead to stern homilies about 'pricing workers out of jobs'.

I want in a moment to look at how this theory stood up to events. But it might be worth first recalling briefly some of the aspects of monetarist thought which most mainstream economists would criticize. Their reservations add up to Sir Ian Gilmour's memorable definition of monetarism as 'the uncontrollable in pursuit of the indefinable'.

For a start, most critics would argue that it is very hard to know in what sense money can be controlled. Which definition ought the government to pick? Should it choose the narrowest measure − M1 − made up mainly of notes and coins and private sector current accounts? Or should it concentrate on the wider definition of sterling M3, which also takes in public sector bank accounts, deposit accounts and sterling certificates of deposit? If bank deposit accounts are included, why not building society accounts? What happens if the main measures move in different directions? This was an important question for policy makers in 1980−1 and in 1981−2. In the first year, sterling M3 rose by 22 per cent, while M1 rose by only 9 per cent. In the second, sterling M3 rose by $13\frac{1}{2}$ per cent, while M1 rose by 8 per cent (see Figure 1). Was monetary policy disturbingly lax − or adequately tight? The one thing which was certain was that, as the economist Charles Goodhart at the Bank of England had pointed out, a measure which is used as a control will change its meaning and so become misleading. [4]

Second, even if the government decides which measure of monetary growth to control, it may run into problems with influencing it. High interest rates are virtually inevitable at some stage for a government using monetary policy to reduce inflation. The problem is that the money supply is not simply determined by the government or by the banks. It depends on what the public is prepared to hold at current rates of interest.

Figure 1 Monetary growth (% change on year earlier)

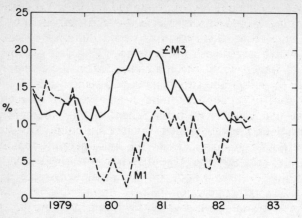

Notes: 1 Based on banking months
2 Adjusted to take account of the introduction of the new monetary sector in November 1981 in place of the former banking sector

Source: Financial Statement and Budget Report 1983–4, HM Treasury, March 1983

It is through high interest rates that the government attracts genuine savings to finance its borrowing in a way which will not add to monetary growth; and through them, too, that private borrowers are supposed to be deterred from borrowing from the banks. But high interest rates can have all sorts of dangerous and perverse side effects.

Third, even if the government does succeed in controlling the money supply, that is not enough. Even the most stringent monetarist would accept that what also matters is velocity: the speed with which money travels round the economy. If that is stable, then there is no problem. Keynesians argue that a monetary squeeze will result in an acceleration of velocity, wiping out much of the impact of the squeeze. To everyone's confusion, the Thatcher monetary squeeze was accompanied (and aggravated) by a sharp fall in velocity. [5]

Finally, and most important, there is still a great deal of argument about the links between monetary growth and inflation. Most monetarists would see one of two connections. At its simplest, they might argue that a rise in money would give people more spending power. That would be reflected in a

4

scramble to buy a limited supply of houses, of stocks and shares and — eventually — of goods and services. The prices of these things would start to rise: as they did, helped on by a general expectation that inflation would continue to rise, workers would start to ask for more pay. The cycle of rising prices and wages would become embedded in the economy long after the initial boost to demand had petered out.

A rather different connection has been developed by economists at the London Business School, from where Mrs Thatcher selected her government's Chief Economic Adviser, Professor Sir Terry Burns. It sees the link operating mainly through the exchange rate. If monetary growth in Britain is faster than elsewhere, money will flow out across the exchanges. The exchange rate will fall, imported goods will become more expensive, and workers will demand more pay to compensate. At the end of the day most of the improvement in competitiveness caused by the devaluation will have been wiped out, leaving prices higher and output much the same as before.

Many non-monetarist economists would accept that monetary growth might, through one or other of these channels, exacerbate inflation during a period of rapid economic expansion. They might argue that a money boom was essentially a symptom of inflationary pressure building up in the labour market, rather than a cause. But they would also argue that the money mechanism did not work symmetrically. If monetary growth contracted, then it might be output which stopped rising — not prices or wages. [6]

To this, most monetarists would reply that a contraction in monetary growth would certainly lead to an initial fall in output and rise in unemployment. Just how serious the fall was would depend on how quickly workers woke up to the fact that the government meant business. Once wages and prices began to stabilize, the fall in inflation would *of itself* be enough to revive the economy. Businessmen would become more confident, interest rates would fall, investment would pick up. The economy, they say, has a powerful tendency to stabilize itself. It does not need endless short-term fine-tuning by governments, tinkering with taxes here and public spending there to keep it on an even keel.

5

And that brings us neatly back to the Medium Term Financial Strategy. For the sceptical observer, it provided two remarkable moments. One was the sight of the government in 1981, in the teeth of an established, home-bred recession, deeper than any since the Second World War, confidently introducing a deflationary budget aimed at reducing public expenditure. The other was the sight of the Chancellor in March 1983, three months away from a General Election, introducing the smallest package of pre-election tax cuts since Roy Jenkins's budget of 1969. (And that was always credited with losing Labour the election of the following year.) The government's belief in the self-stabilizing effect of reduced inflation was being tested to the limit.

But it is time to turn to the government's record. It is possible to interpret it in two ways. If you are a persistent monetarist, you could claim that adherence to the Medium Term Financial Strategy has paid off, and that firm monetary policy has dramatically reduced inflation. If you are more sceptical, you might point out that the most dramatic effect of monetary policy has been to help to deliver three years with an extremely uncompetitive exchange rate; that the recession is the result of an overvalued exchange rate combined with a tough fiscal squeeze; and that the government's success in reducing inflation is the unsurprising result of allowing unemployment to rise to its highest levels for fifty years.

The most remarkable single influence on the economy in the first two years of the Thatcher government was a collapse of international competitiveness. This had two causes. First, the government's first year saw a strong acceleration of inflation, the result of a combination of factors. For instance, there was pressure from the world outside: the rate of world inflation doubled between the last quarter of 1978 and the first quarter of 1979. But the government also made bad errors of judgement. In the first budget, Value Added Tax was almost doubled; and a series of highly inflationary public sector pay settlements were delivered by the Comparability Commission, set up by the previous government. To some extent, the new government suffered the inevitable rebound from the pay policies of its predecessor (see chapter 2, pp. 39–40). This led to prices rising at an annual rate of over 20 per cent and a surge in unit labour costs.

The second factor behind the loss of competitiveness was a strong rise in the exchange rate. Again, there were several reasons for this. One was simply the admiration of foreign bankers for Mrs Thatcher's determined approach and monetary orthodoxy. Another was sterling's new status as a petro-currency at a time when oil prices were rocketing upwards. The fall in activity strengthened the current account. So did North Sea oil, moving it strongly into surplus, at a time when other countries were having to export more just to meet their existing oil needs. But with hindsight, the most important single factor was almost certainly the sharp rise in interest rates which was the concomitant of the government's monetary squeeze.

The net result of the sterling appreciation was a sharp deterioration in competitiveness. Unit labour costs in manufacturing, relative to those in other countries, rose by some 50 per cent in the three years to 1981. And this rise in the 'real' exchange rate (as opposed to the nominal rate — the thing foreign exchange dealers quote) was arguably inevitable. For in a world of freely floating exchange rates, with a vast market in highly mobile international capital, the behaviour of both the real and the nominal exchange rate may have precious little to do with the movement of the current account — the trade figures which we all used to watch so anxiously (see Figure 2). The behaviour of the nominal rate, as the figure shows, may not even have much effect in offsetting changes in domestic costs, as most people once believed.

A more immediate influence on the exchange rate seems to be monetary policy. Tight money promptly drives up the exchange rate — because it raises interest rates: and because the labour market responds much more slowly as it takes longer to change the trend labour costs, the result is a big loss of competitiveness. This sort of 'overshooting' has not only affected sterling. In the two years after monetary policy was sharply tightened in the United States in the summer of 1980, the real dollar exchange rate appreciated by 30 per cent.

As interest rates began to fall in the UK, the nominal exchange rate also began to weaken. Labour costs began rising slowly. There was an increase in productivity, unusual at this stage of a recession. But as the onset of the international

Figure 2 Real exchange rates[1]

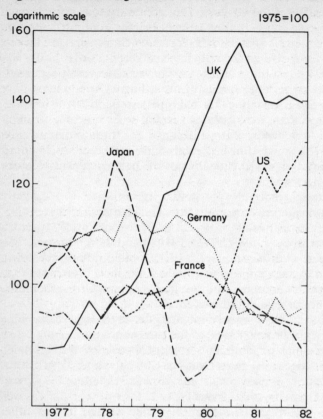

Logarithmic scale   1975=100

Note: 1 Exchange rates adjusted for changes in normalized unit labour costs

Source: *Bank of England Quarterly Bulletin*, September 1982, p. 334

recession meant that labour costs in other countries were also
levelling off, not all of the UK's loss of competitiveness was
retrieved. By the beginning of 1983, sterling's real exchange
rate was still more than 20 per cent above its 1975–9 average.
It was not until the further decline in the early months of 1983
that competitiveness finally returned more or less to its trend
levels. [7]

The impact of this loss of competitiveness abroad, coupled
with extremely high interest rates at home, was to concentrate

the full force of the squeeze on manufacturing companies. They suffered in two ways. They continued to export as much – or even more – than before. Britain went into recession before the rest of the world: for many firms, foreign markets must have offered the only hope of keeping order books up. But profits on those orders must have been severely squeezed. (At the same time, foreign firms selling to Britain must have found the game money for old rope.) Secondly, British manufacturers found the cost of keeping stocks became prohibitively high. Most companies pay for their stock of raw materials, partly-finished goods and finished products out of borrowed money. When the cost of borrowing is driven up, their first reaction is to cut back on stocks.

And this, indeed, is precisely what happened. In 1980 there was a staggering turnround from stockbuilding to destocking. There was a further sharp decline in stocks in 1981, and a smaller drop in 1982. Taking 1980 and 1981 together, you arrive at a cumulative figure of £5.2 billion. A turnround in stocks of such dimensions would alone have been more than enough to account for the sharp fall in Gross Domestic Product over the same period. [8, 9]

There is, then, quite a lot of evidence to suggest that high interest rates contributed to the recession. There is quite a lot of evidence, too, for a powerful fiscal squeeze. What is much harder to trace is direct evidence of slow monetary growth.

As I have already remarked (see page 3), sterling M3 grew at a brisk pace in 1980–1 and 1981–2. In both years, it was well above the targets the Chancellor had set for it. But other measures of money suggest that there may have been a ferocious monetary squeeze. In 1982–3 there was a significant relaxation of monetary policy: the target range for growth was set at 8 to 12 per cent, instead of the 5 to 9 per cent figures in earlier versions of the MTFS. There were other signs of disenchantment. The government announced its intention to add two new measures of money to its target range (M1 and PSL2 – a wider definition of private sector liquidity). And it promised that in some unspecified way, monetary policy would 'take account of all the available evidence', including the exchange rate.

The course of fiscal policy is rather easier to trace. The 1980

Budget was clearly deflationary in conventional terms. (To the government, which saw the main hindrance to economic growth as inflation, anything which reduced the public sector's need to borrow could hardly be called 'deflationary'.) But orthodox economists looked on in some horror as the Chancellor announced plans to reduce the ratio of the budget deficit from about 3.6 per cent of Gross Domestic Product to 3 per cent, while at the same time forecasting a decline of $2\frac{1}{2}$ per cent in output.

In practice, the budget deficit for 1980–1 turned out to be £11 billion, compared with the target of £7 billion. The net impact on the economy had been broadly neutral. But the 1981 Budget was even more deflationary in intent. It aimed to cut the deficit by £$5\frac{1}{2}$ billion, at a time when output was again expected to fall (this time by 2 per cent). This time, the government more than succeeded. The deficit was actually slightly below target. So was the deficit for 1982–3, although the stance in the 1982 Budget was broadly neutral. Only in the 1983 Budget, with an election clearly on the horizon, did the Conservative government produce its first non-deflationary package.

But all these bits of 'conventional' arithmetic ignore two facts, both of which make the real impact of the Thatcher fiscal policy more severe than it appears. First, they make no allowance for the decline in Gross Domestic Product through the period. As output fell – and unemployment rose – the size of the budget deficit would normally have risen. After all, public expenditure was swollen by social security payments, and tax receipts were reduced as people earned less income and companies made less profits. Had employment remained constant, then the cumulative tightening of fiscal policy would undoubtedly have been greater.

Conventional measures of fiscal policy do not only ignore the effect of changes in the level of employment. They also ignore the effects of inflation. While companies and their accountants have been arguing for a decade about ways of presenting company accounts to extract the distorting effects of inflation on profits, the government has shown no such interest in the presentation of its accounts. But rapid inflation forces the government to pay very high levels of nominal interest on its new debt. Adjust those interest payments (which account for a large chunk of total public spending) for inflation, and the public sector borrowing requirement was probably small in 1980–1 and in surplus the following year. In other words, in a world without inflation, the government would have been shown to be pursuing a budget surplus in the teeth of the worst recession since the War.

The justification for this, in the eyes of Mrs Thatcher and her ministers, would be the remarkable decline in inflation. Part of the reason for this decline has been a dramatic improvement in the behaviour of unit labour costs. They rose, in the eighteen months to spring 1983, by less than the OECD average for the first time in ten years. This in part reflected a rise in productivity. But it was also helped along by the slower rise in wages as unemployment increased — and by the long period of a strong exchange rate.

The real question now is what will happen as recovery gradually takes place. The government has been disappointed by the time it has taken for the economy to show signs of spontaneous revival. Flickers of life early in 1982 misled Sir Geoffrey Howe into confident statements in his Budget about 'the recovery we foresaw and worked for is now taking place'. Luck was not on his side: the big collapse in world activity took place in the second half of 1982 and helped to dampen any revival in the UK.

But suppose the recovery does take off. The prospects, as of spring 1983, have undoubtedly been improved by the sharp fall in world oil prices, and by signs of revival in the United States. If monetary policy is kept within the target range, regardless of what is happening to inflation or to Gross National Product, will not the recovery bring a new monetary squeeze with higher interest rates driving the exchange rate up again, and choking off revival? And if by contrast monetary policy is rather relaxed, will there be a sharp new upturn of inflation? Some pressure on prices has clearly been built up with the fall in the exchange rate in late 1982 and early 1983. But what about wages? Have the inflationary expectations of workers finally been ground into dust? Or will the tightening of the labour market, even against the background of more than three million unemployed, result in a gradual rise in the

11

level of pay settlements? Certainly that is the outturn on which I would put my money. With Mrs Thatcher's experiment not yet completed, the case for attributing the decline of inflation to a strong exchange rate and an old-fashioned international recession looks more powerful than the case for successful monetarism. [10]

Questions

[1] Framework for the control of the money supply

The framework within which the UK government seeks to contain the money supply was the subject of the chapter 'Running the economy: how much does money matter?' in the first *Guardian Guide to the Economy*. The framework is still appropriate.

[2] Inflationary expectations, part one

Current economic thinking about inflation is powerfully influenced by the work of Milton Friedman. It is no longer acceptable to write glibly about 'cost push' and 'demand pull'. Friedman's main insight was to argue that the inflationary process can be divided into two distinct components:

inflation = expected inflation + demand inflation

He argued that once inflation started, people built it into their economic decisions about wage claims, price increases and so on.

But where does the inflation come from to start with? Friedman explains this through the notion of the natural rate of unemployment — which he defines as being the level of unemployment associated with zero price inflation. If the government seeks to reduce this level of unemployment it will do so only at the cost of increasing inflation.* This inflation is referred to as demand inflation.

Friedman then inserts the 'special case' where:

expected inflation = last year's inflation

and develops three critical propositions on the basis of this.

Proposition 1

This starts with a situation in Year 1 where there is 6% unemployment and 0% price inflation. The government decides that the level of unemployment is unacceptable and so it introduces a reflationary package which reduces unemployment to 4% but raises inflation to 2%. In Year 3 that demand inflation gets built into people's expectations.

i Work out and complete the process which now follows:

Year	Expected inflation	Demand inflation	Unemployment	Actual inflation
1	0	0	6	0
2	0	2	4	2
3	2	2	4	
4		2		
5		2		

From this Friedman's first proposition is:

Higher inflation will not reduce unemployment permanently; only accelerating inflation can do this.

Proposition 2

In Year 6 the government becomes concerned over the rising rate of inflation and so it decides to deflate the economy. This it does over two years, allowing unemployment to revert to its natural level with demand inflation reducing to zero in Year 7.

* Friedman does not say, therefore, that the natural rate is inevitable – only that the government cannot reduce it by increasing demand. It could instead try to improve the way the job market works.

ii   Record the course of the economy until Year 10.

Year	Expected inflation	Demand inflation	Unemployment	Actual inflation
6	8	1	5	
7		0	6	
8		0	6	
9		0	6	
10		0	6	

From this we have Friedman's second proposition:

> To maintain a constant rate of inflation, unemployment must equal the natural rate.

Proposition 3

In Year 11 the government determines to reduce the level of inflation by further cutting the level of demand and exerting deflationary pressure on the economy.

iii   What will now happen to inflation?

Year	Expected inflation	Demand inflation	Unemployment	Actual inflation
11	9	−2	8	
12		−2		
13		−2		
14		−2		

The third proposition is:

> To reduce inflation, unemployment must rise above the natural rate.

iv   To what extent do you think Friedman's three 'special case' propositions might provide an interpretation of UK economic experience 1959–83?

[3] Inflationary expectations, part two

As in all economics the critical number is one. Friedman's three propositions assume a coefficient of inflationary expectations of one (which only means that if inflation was 10% last year we assume it will be 10% this year).

Peter Shore, as the Labour Shadow Chancellor, argued that Friedman's explanation of the inflationary process is quite right but that the coefficient of expected inflation is less than 1 — let us call it $\frac{1}{2}$.

i What will, therefore, occur if Mr Shore were correct and the government reflates the economy to drive down unemployment?

Year	Expected inflation	Demand inflation	Unemploy-ment	Actual inflation
1	0	0	6	0
2	0	2	4	2
3	1	2	4	
4		2	4	
5		2	4	

It is of course perfectly possible that both Messrs Friedman and Shore are being too conservative and that the coefficient of expected inflation is much higher — say 2. In this case if inflation was 5% last year we anticipate it will be 10% this year.

ii You can now explore the consequences of a reflationary programme, with the expectations coefficient at 2.

Year	Expected inflation	Demand inflation	Unemploy-ment	Actual inflation
1	0	0	6	0
2	0	2	4	2
3	4	2	4	
4		0	6	
5		0	6	
6		−5	11	
7		−10	16	

iii   What did the government do in Years 4, 6 and 7; what effect did this have upon the economy?

The crucial problem is the value of the coefficient of expected inflation:

iv   Do you, first of all, think it is rational to argue that people anticipate price changes in the way Friedman asserts?

Assume the coefficient of expected inflation is 1 but that recorded levels of inflation are:

Year	Actual inflation
1	0
2	2
3	4
4	6
5	8

v   What would you expect to happen to people's inflationary expectations?

vi   What do you think the current coefficient of expected inflation is for the UK economy? What implications does this have for government policy?

[4]   The UK monetary aggregates

Table 1 shows the compositions of the main UK monetary aggregates.

The chapter draws attention to the fact that during the period of MTFS the monetary aggregates were prone to behave in conflicting ways. It became difficult to know the rate of increase of the 'money supply' because the rate depended upon the aggregate measure adopted.

i   On the assumption that people will put their savings where they get the best rate of interest, what will happen to each of the monetary aggregates if the rate of interest offered by the banks on deposit accounts rises substantially?

Table 1 The UK monetary aggregates

	M1	M2	£M3[1]	PSL1	PSL2
A. Notes and coin	x	x	x	x	x
B. Bank deposits					
1. Maturity and interest					
a) Non-interest bearing sight deposits	x	x	x	x	x
b) Interest bearing checkable deposits	x	x	x	x	x
c) Other interest bearing sight deposits	x		x	x	x
d) Time deposits[2] of less than one month		x	x	x	x
e) Time deposits[2] of one month to two years			x	x	x
f) Time deposits[2] of over two years			x		
2. Sector of depositor					
a) UK private sector	x	x	x	x	x
b) UK public sector			x		
3. Size of deposit					
a) Less than £100,000	x	x	x	x	x
b) £100,000 and over	x		x	x	x
C. Other money market instruments[3]				x	x
D. Savings deposits and securities[4]					x

[1] M3 is the same as £M3, but includes foreign currency deposits of UK non-bank residents
[2] Including Certificates of Deposit
[3] Treasury Bills, Certificates of tax deposit, bank bills, deposits with local authorities and finance houses
[4] Shares and deposits with building societies, National Savings Bank deposits, and National Savings securities, excluding all assets not realizable within a year without significant loss. Includes Trustee Savings Bank deposits to November 1981, but since then they have been reclassified as bank deposits within the new monetary sector.

Source: *Lloyds Bank Economic Bulletin*, August 1982 (The *Bulletin* is available to schools free of charge. Write to Group Economics Department, Lloyds Bank PLC, 71 Lombard St, London EC3P 3BS.)

ii   *What will happen if the rate of interest on building society share accounts rose to a level where it was 3% or 4% above bank deposit rate?*

iii   *M2 is known as 'retail deposits' – what do all its constituent parts have in common which leads to this tag being given to it?*

iv   Why is it important to have a measure of what may be called transaction balances as opposed to broader measures of the money stock?

[5]   The velocity of circulation

Any policy which regards control of the money supply as being the main determinant of the level of economic activity has its intellectual origins in Fisher's Quantity Theory of Money:

$$MV = PT$$

With the velocity of circulation fixed in the short-run and with the tendency for the economy to be sluggish in terms of increasing output in the short-run, it is tempting to argue that V and T do not alter, and so the identity should be written as:

$$M\overline{V} = P\overline{T}$$

Thus any increase in the stock of money would raise money expenditure but the increase in nominal income could only occur as a rise in prices. It would be equally tempting to argue that reductions in the stock of money will reduce nominal income by bringing prices down.

Figure 3   The velocity of circulation (ratio of GNP at market prices to £M3)

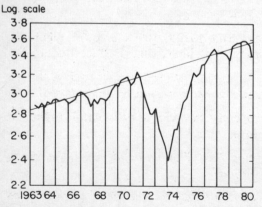

Source: S. Brittan, 'How to end the "monetarist" controversy', Institute of Economic Affairs, Hobart Paper 90, Second edition 1982

Once the assumption about the stability of the velocity of circulation is withdrawn, however, the identity becomes less predictable. The evidence that the velocity of circulation in the UK is not particularly stable is shown in Figure 3.

i   *What is the velocity of circulation and how is it measured?*

ii   *Money expenditure = Nominal income. How would this normally be written?*

iii   *The most dramatic recent rise in the UK money supply was in 1971–3 (see Figure 4, p. 20). What happened to money expenditure?*

iv   *What might happen in an economy if the money supply growth was suddenly reduced?*

[6]   Money GDP

One of the customary areas of weakness in students' economics essays is the failure to stress that the money value of output is the product of real output multiplied by the price level. If the level of aggregate demand in an economy is increased, then GDP (Y in the circular flow model) may be seen to rise, but:

the crucial issue is whether it is the price element or the real output element which changes.

In his highly recommended study (see source for Figure 3), Samuel Brittan produces an interesting chart (see Figure 4).

i   *In a paragraph, explain the phrase, 'Gross Domestic Product at current market prices, expenditure based'.*

ii   *What was the average annual rate of inflation in the UK from 1974 to 1979?*

iii   *During the period 1959–79 what happened to the rate of growth of real output?*

iv   *Money GDP (or nominal income or Y in Keynesian models) rose by 128.9% during the period covered; what happened to real income?*

19

Figure 4 The growth of money GDP (Gross Domestic Product at current market prices, expenditure based)

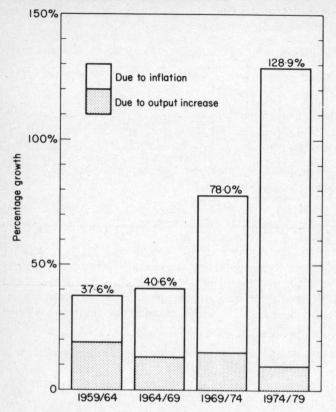

[7] Loss of competitiveness (see Figure 5)

i   What does a loss of competitiveness mean and how is it affected by a falling exchange rate?

ii   How can unit labour costs be reduced if money wages keep rising?

[8] Destocking

Working on the basis that firms produce output in advance of demand, we can consider the following figures for an

Figure 5 Changes in competitiveness: December 1982 compared to the average of 1973–80

Loss in competitiveness (%)

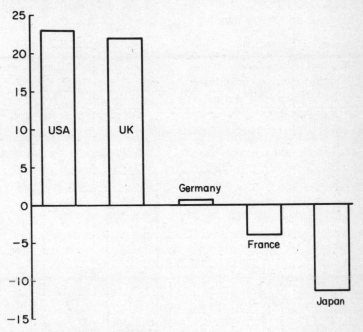

Source: *World Financial Markets*

economy (which for the sake of simplicity we assume to be closed).

Year 1
GDP = £113 billion
Taxation = £40 billion
Consumer expenditure = £61 billion
Private sector investment = £18 billion
Public sector expenditure = £34 billion
Private sector savings = £12 billion

i *Using a conventional circular flow model, check that this economy is in an equilibrium condition.*

Year 2

This sees a substantial increase in the rate of interest and an increased fear of unemployment. The level of output has again been set at £113 billion by the production decisions of firms. Private sector savings, however, rise by £5 billion.

GDP =
Taxation =
Consumer expenditure =
Private sector investment =
Public sector expenditure =
Private sector savings =

ii   Record what you think will happen in the economy as a consequence of the reduced level of consumer expenditure.

Year 3

Firms decide to reduce the level of stocks for two reasons – the high interest rate cost of holding them and the increase unexpectedly experienced as a consequence of the reduction in consumer demand last year. Their decision is to reduce stocks by £8 billion. The multiplier for this economy is thought to be about 1.47.

iii   Explain what will happen in this economy. If you assume that all average propensities remain unchanged, you should be able to ascertain the new equilibrium level and complete the table below:

GDP =
Taxation =
Consumer expenditure =
Private sector investment =
Public sector expenditure =
Private sector savings =

[9]   Destocking in the UK economy

See Table 2 on page 23.

Why did Gross Domestic Product of the UK economy at 1975 prices fall from £116 billion in 1979 to £113 billion in 1982?

Table 2 Expenditure on the Gross Domestic Product, 1975 prices (seasonally adjusted)

| | Gross Domestic Product | | Final expenditure on goods and services at market prices (£ million) | | | | | | | |
	At market prices	At factor cost	Total final expenditure	Consumers' expenditure	General government consumption	Gross domestic fixed capital formation	Value of physical increase in stocks and work in progress	Exports of goods and services	Imports of goods and services	Adjustment to factor cost
1976	108,544	97,793	138,778	64,707	22,178	20,640	658	29,595	30,234	10,751
1977	109,935	99,190	140,497	64,517	22,951	20,139	1,382	31,508	30,562	10,745
1978	113,989	102,279	145,743	68,227	23,438	20,839	1,147	32,092	31,754	11,710
1979	115,886	103,723	151,212	71,599	23,866	21,041	1,792	32,914	35,326	12,163
1980	113,696	101,521	147,785	71,582	24,311	20,426	-1,568	33,034	34,089	12,175
1981	111,277	99,140	145,180	71,869	24,315	18,617	-1,885	32,264	33,903	12,137
1982	112,873	100,532	148,409	72,658	24,782	19,280	-808	32,497	35,536	12,341
1981 1	28,213	25,049	35,938	18,024	6,055	4,643	-670	7,886	7,725	3,164
2	27,643	24,702	35,889	17,944	6,054	4,636	-740	7,995	8,246	2,941
3	27,460	24,503	36,552	17,921	6,131	4,620	-240	8,120	9,092	2,957
4	27,961	24,886	36,801	17,980	6,075	4,718	-235	8,263	8,840	3,075
1982 1	28,108	24,983	36,981	17,901	6,159	4,844	-46	8,123	8,873	3,125
2	27,903	24,981	37,065	18,002	6,174	4,654	-34	8,269	9,162	2,922
3	28,147	25,059	36,939	18,239	6,230	4,898	-323	7,895	8,792	3,088
4	28,715	25,509	37,424	18,516	6,219	4,884	-405	8,210	8,709	3,206

Source: Central Statistical Office, press release, 29 March 1983

[10] The shape of the aggregate supply curve

In 1979 the Conservative government embarked upon the policy of reducing total expenditure within the economy in an attempt to control inflation. Expansion of aggregate demand during the preceding years had the effect of increasing the rate of inflation. What would now happen to the composition of nominal income if demand was contracted? Would the effect be felt in terms of reduced prices or reduced real output?

Posing this question is not dissimilar to the classic microeconomic question:

'What happens in a market if demand falls?'

Like all answers in economics it starts with 'It all depends on. . . .' We can apply the same means of analysis here:

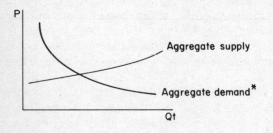

i   If the government acts in this situation to shift the level of aggregate demand (or money expenditure) to the left − what will happen in the economy?

ii   How would you describe the shape of the aggregate supply curve in this case?

iii   What would be the consequences of shifting demand downwards in an economy displaying the characteristics shown in the figure on p. 25?

---

* The aggregate demand curve is more properly shown as a curve of unit elasticity; the reasons for this need not concern us here but an excellent detailed explanation and more thorough exposition of this analysis appears in *Modern Economic Analysis 2*, D. H. Gowland (ed.), Butterworth, 1982.

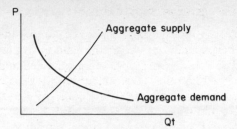

Notice that in this analysis it does not matter what means are used to reduce the level of aggregate demand, defined as money expenditure. You can adopt what textbooks would call 'Keynesian' techniques: reducing public expenditure, raising taxation, increasing rates of interest to deter consumer finance and investment. Or you can pursue 'monetarist' approaches: controlling the rate of growth of the MS, allowing the interest rate pattern to move upwards. As the chapter points out, they are much the same! What matters is the assumed shape of the aggregate supply curve, because this dictates how the composition of nominal income will change in response to the change in demand.

This simple model can explain the different perceptions of economic policy early in 1983 and the reasons for the fury of the argument:

iv *Peter Shore argued for a substantial reflation of total expenditure and insisted that the inflationary increase in nominal income would be minimal. Produce a diagram showing the expansionary shift in aggregate demand and the shape of the supply curve assumed by Mr Shore.*

v *Sir Geoffrey Howe as Chancellor of the Exchequer insisted that any expansion of demand would be dangerously inflationary and would undo 'the sacrifices of recent years'. What sort of aggregate supply curve does this assume?*

vi *Who saw the aggregate supply having the properties shown in the figure on p. 26? What does the range a-b denote?*

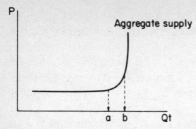

P

Aggregate supply

a b   Qt

vii A market supply curve shows the response suppliers make to changes in price brought about by changes in demand.
   a What determines the shape of a market supply curve?
   b What factors are likely to determine the shape of the aggregate supply curve for the UK economy?
   c Can the shape of the supply curve − the economy's supply responses − be affected by government policy?

Further reading

For general reading *The UK Economy* (A. R. Prest and D. J. Coppock (eds), Weidenfeld & Nicolson, 1982) is a more academic and rigorous approach to the problems discussed throughout this book. A bit less easy to understand − but still accessible to the non-specialist.

The best regular commentaries on current economic policy are:

1 The *Bank of England Quarterly Bulletin* (but closely reflects official views, although the Bank's are sometimes visible between the lines; available from the Economics Division, Bank of England, London EC2R 8AH. The 1983 subscription rate is £8 and this includes the excellent digest, 'Bank Briefing', which is a veritable treasure trove of data response material.)

2 The *Economic Review* of the National Institute of Economic and Social Research (strongly Keynesian; available

quarterly from the NIESR at 2 Dean Trench St, London SW1. The annual subscription rate to schools and students is £10.)

3 *Economic Outlook* ('broadly' monetarist; published quarterly by the Centre for Economic Forecasting, London Business School, Sussex Place, Regents Park, London NW1.)

The best review of Mrs Thatcher's economic policies is *The Thatcher Experiment: an Interim Report* by Willem Buiter and Marcus Miller (first published in *Brookings Papers on Economic Activity*, no. 1, 1981, and republished as Centre for Labour Economics Discussion Paper 106, London School of Economics, December 1981. An updated version will be published in *Brookings Papers on Economic Activity*, no. 1, 1984.)

The best City comment on the current situation is usually in Morgan Grenfell's *Economic Review* (available free from Morgan Grenfell & Co. Ltd, 23 Great Winchester St, London EC2).

2 Pay – what determines it?

Right at the heart of economic management is the behaviour of pay. In most industries, pay is the principle cost of production (and for most households, it is the main source of income). So the amount which a company's workers are paid has a big effect on the ability of that company to compete with its rivals, at home and in the export markets. Moreover, if people want their pay to go up faster than the value of the goods they produce increases, the result is usually inflation – rising prices.

British governments since the Second World War have been chiefly preoccupied with two economic issues – international competitiveness and inflation. The second has gradually overtaken the first, although as I argue in the next chapter, a lot of the new debate about deindustrialization is really the old debate about competitiveness. But both issues have led governments to look for ways of influencing pay. As we saw in the last chapter, the Conservative government under Mrs Thatcher has tried to influence pay indirectly, through monetary policy. But most post-war British governments have resorted sooner or later to incomes policy.

This chapter examines the reasons why pay has proved so difficult for governments to influence. A large part of the answer lies in the way the structure of pay rates is determined. For to the extent that pay rates are fixed by supply and demand, any attempt to alter them without first changing the supply of a particular skill or the demand for it will be doomed to failure. To the extent that pay is determined by social factors – by convention or by concepts of status or notions of what is fair – pay rates may be malleable.

There are, of course, two separate points here – and indeed, in trying to influence pay, governments have often been trying to do two separate jobs at once. There is the question of how the pay for one job is fixed relative to another. And there is the question of how the pay bill for the workforce as a whole is determined. But the two issues are closely related. For any attempt to alter the overall rate at which pay increases – particularly through direct action such as incomes policy – will almost inevitably alter the structure of differentials. And that, some would argue, is the essential reason why incomes policy has proved so unsuccessful.

The question of why some people are paid more for what they do than others has been perplexing economists for three centuries. Pay, after all, is a sort of price. If it were like the price of tomatoes, it would respond mainly to the pressures of supply and demand. If the skill which a particular worker had was suddenly in greater demand, the amount which employers or customers would be willing to pay for it would rise. The rise in pay would encourage more workers to move into the job or acquire the skill – and eventually, the relative pay would fall back again to a point where there were just enough workers with enough skill to meet the demands of employers or customers at a price with which they were happy. Something very like this seems to have happened with computer programmers: in the first flush of enthusiasm for computers, programmers' pay was high relative to what someone with similar skills could earn elsewhere. But becoming a programmer did not take very long, and soon the market became crowded and the relative pay of computer programmers declined.

But the workings of supply and demand in the job market are tempered by all sorts of social rigidities. People rarely change their occupation in mid-career. Children have a disproportionate tendency to do what their parents did. People find it difficult to move house to another part of the country where there are more jobs available – particularly if they live in a council house which cannot be sold. Sometimes the forces which pen people into a particular job are even less rational: think how few black bank managers there are, or women car mechanics.

These constraints on the ability of people to pick whichever job they wanted struck the economist John Stuart Mill more than a century ago, when he was looking for an explanation for that most perplexing of labour market enigmas, the fact that the nastiest jobs are the worst paid. He saw that if the only factor which affected the number of people who wanted a particular job was whether or not it was pleasant to do, nasty jobs would be better paid than nice ones. But, he went on, 'The really exhausting and the really repulsive labours, instead of being better paid than others, are almost invariably paid the worst of all, because performed by those who have no choice.' That last phrase − 'performed by those who have no choice' − was developed by another Victorian economist, John Cairnes, into the concept of non-competing industrial groups. Once trained, he argued, workers did not often move between occupations. It was young workers who responded to changes in demand. But the choice open even to a youngster was limited by social background which tended to constrain the sons and daughters of unskilled workers to unskilled jobs, and encourage the children of professional men to find work in another profession. Cairnes produced a vivid metaphor: 'What we find, in effect, is not a whole population competing indiscriminately for all occupations, but a series of industrial layers, superimposed on one another, within each of which the various candidates for employment possess a real and effective power of selection while those occupying the several strata are, for all purposes of effective competition, practically isolated from each other.'

What Cairnes is saying is that the supply of labour can only respond in a very slow and inadequate way to changes in demand. I will come back to the constraints on mobility in a moment: they are clearly very powerful, not just in Britain but in all Western societies. But the other side of the job market is also enmeshed in rigidities. Employers quite clearly do not always signal that they are short of a particular skill by raising its relative pay − and hardly ever signal that they have too much of a particular kind of worker by widening a differential. The large wages of London printers certainly do not mean that the newspapers need more of them. And the fact that London is perennially short of traffic wardens is conveyed to the market by advertising vacancies, not by paying wardens as much as policemen.

Some economists have been so impressed by these rigidities that they have come to doubt whether demand and supply really have any impact that matters on rates of pay. The closer one examines the forces which immediately determine what people are paid, the more conscious one becomes of the compartmentalized inflexibility of the job market. [1]

Simply examining the differential rates paid for similar jobs in different firms poses some interesting questions. Occupation is the most obvious reason for differences in pay: we expect barristers to earn more than clerks, and divers in the North Sea to earn more than swimming pool attendants. But within one occupation, pay can vary enormously. The spread of industrial earnings of manual workers in any one occupation is usually almost as wide as the spread between the lowest average earnings in any manual occupation and the highest − almost 2 to 1.

Dr Guy Routh has put together a monumental study of the links between occupations and pay for this century (*Occupation and Pay in Great Britain 1906−79*, Macmillan, 1980). He found that in 1978 the worst paid 10 per cent of general managers in the mechanical engineering industry were paid an average of £76 a week. The best paid 10 per cent were paid an average of £310 a week. For other occupations in engineering the range was less dramatic, but still impressive. For instance, the worst paid 10 per cent of women secretaries and shorthand typists working full-time in engineering firms earned an average of £42.20 a week. The best paid 10 per cent earned £69.40 a week. It is clearly fairly meaningless to talk about the average pay for a general manager or a secretary, even in something as confined as the engineering industry.

Not only does pay vary between very similar jobs in a single industry. It can vary strikingly for similar jobs in similar firms in a single industry in a single town. Dr Routh quotes a report by Derek Robinson, deputy chairman of the Pay Board in 1973−4, of a seminar in Oxford which bears out this point. The seminar, he said, found 'many examples of pairs of plants in the same locality engaged on very similar engineering work where the higher paying firm, which also had better fringe benefits and physical surroundings, had a lower rate of productivity. It has not been possible to test this relationship in any systematic and quantifiable way, but there are strong general impressions that the money and effort bargains of

31

members of the same occupation in the same industry in the same town are by no means similar. Indeed, the relationship is often reversed, so that lower paying firms may have a higher rate of productivity' (p. 218). [2]

There are, of course, some logical explanations for wide differences of pay within a single occupation. To go back to the previous point, the term general manager — and the term secretary — cover a wide range of responsibilities. Pay tends to rise with responsibility and indeed with age. But the evidence suggests that an individual company or even a plant may have a pay structure of its own which is only loosely tied to that of similar firms in the same town, and which delivers differentials which are only partly explicable in terms of the shortage of a particular skill and the abilities which a particular job demands.

These differentials would no doubt be narrower if workers moved more freely from one employer to another — or indeed from one occupation to another. But the evidence suggests that after a certain age, people rarely change their jobs. One of the most succinct studies of movement between occupations is by Professor David Metcalf, who was particularly interested in the causes of low pay (*Low Pay, Occupational Mobility, and Minimum-Wage Policy in Britain*, American Enterprise Institute for Public Policy Research, 1150 17th Street NW, Washington, DC 20036). He found that most people remain in the occupation they first enter for all their working lives. Of people who were in the worst paid 10 per cent of occupations in 1965, two-thirds (65 per cent) were still there ten years later. Some occupations seem to be easier to move out of than others. Chefs, bus conductors and motor drivers were, he found, all quite likely to move into a better paid occupation. But hardly any people in agricultural occupations — farm workers, stockmen, operators of agricultural machinery — were likely to better themselves. [3]

David Metcalf then went on to look at the effect age had on job changes. He found that almost all the teenagers in the worst paid tenth of occupations moved into something better paid in the course of ten years. But more than half of those aged between 20 and 34 stayed put at the bottom of the ladder — as did 80 per cent of those aged over 35. The depressing moral is that the occupation you are in by the end of your teens is very likely to be the one in which you spend your working life: and once you have done something for twenty years, you are most unlikely to break out into something with better prospects.

'The implication of this should not be misconstrued,' says Professor Metcalf. 'It does not imply that if we take a random school leaver and somehow or other place him in a high ranked occupation he will then be set up for life. All this . . . shows is that the underlying personal characteristics and social forces which determine the individual's initial position continue to operate through his life.' The characteristics which people have and acquire before they even join the workforce play a large part in determining the kind of occupation in which they spend most of their life.

More is known about these links for men than for women. The most important recent study was carried out by Professor Richard Layard and a team of colleagues for the Royal Commission on the Distribution of Income and Wealth (*The Causes of Poverty*, by R. Layard, D. Piachaud and M. Stewart in collaboration with N. Barr, A. Cornford and B. Hayes, Background Paper to Report No. 6: Lower Incomes, HMSO). One of the most important influences on hourly earnings, this study estimated, was the number of years spent in full-time education. A man who left school at 15 earns an 11 per cent premium over one who left at the age of 14; and on average, each year of education beyond the age of 14 adds 9 per cent to pay. Qualifications also deliver extra earning power. Layard and his team calculated that a man with the City and Guilds Final craft qualification got a 25 per cent premium over one with no qualifications, and that a man with a degree earned, other things equal, roughly double as much as someone with no qualification. [4]

Extra years of education and training might be regarded as investment in a sort of human capital, on which an individual might expect to earn a return over a lifetime of work. Why would anyone bother to go to university − except for a brief holiday between school and work − unless three or four years of extra study offered some hope of a better paid job at the end of the day? But the lead times on investment in human capital may be very long. If (say) the discovery of oil in the North Sea creates a big new demand for geology graduates with experience of management and special knowledge of underwater prospecting, it may take several years before the market delivers the goods.

It is easy to see why years of work experience, or education, or qualifications result in higher hourly earnings: they raise the value of the hourly output of the individual worker. But other influences are not so justifiable. A person's colour patently affects his earning power: the Layard paper found that the gap between a white man who left school at 14 and one born in the West Indies was around 13 per cent. The persistent gap between the earnings of women and of men is also only partly explicable. Once you have allowed for the interruption in the work experience of women who have children, for the concentration of women in less skilled jobs and for the fact that they are less likely to earn premiums for overtime, there is still a hard core of difference which is only explicable in term of sex discrimination.

Some factors seem to predispose people to earn more than others. Family background clearly makes a difference; though how far your parents contribute to your earnings by determining your choice of job (doctors' children are more likely than others to become doctors), how far by influencing your educational experience (the children of manual workers are less likely to stay on at school than the children of managers) and how far in more nebulous, unmeasurable ways (like passing on their brains or their *savoir faire*) is unknown and probably always will be.

But there are also factors which affect what people earn after they have found a job. The most striking is simply their work experience. Earnings go up rapidly with the number of years spent at work – at least well into middle age. And workers depreciate rapidly. One study found that women who stopped working to have children lost 3 per cent of their potential earning power with every year they stayed at home (A. Zabalza and T. Zannatos, unpublished report for the Equal Opportunities Commission). [5]

Another influence on what people earn after they have found a job is membership of a trade union. All the main studies of the impact of trade union membership on pay find that union members enjoy some sort of premium over those who are not in a union. But there is some disagreement about how big the premium is, and whether unions are responsible for it. Studies of male manual workers in the mid-1970s suggested that men covered by collective agreements might earn between 12 and 25 per cent more than men who were not covered. It is also possible that trade unions prefer organizing the better paid: their employers are a more gentlemanly lot, and they tend to work in bigger companies. That makes life easier for the organizer.

There are a number of other problems with arriving at a reasonable estimate of the impact of union membership on pay. First, the threat of unionization may persuade some employers (Marks and Spencer?) to pay their workers more than they otherwise would. Secondly, employers who are forced by trade unions to pay higher wages to their employees than they otherwise would may, as a result, be able to attract better quality workers. That in turn may improve their productivity. Once that happens, of course, the cost of the union mark-up to the employer is reduced. [6]

A more interesting effect of the spread of trade unions has been to reduce the variations in the earnings of their members. As early as 1902 Sidney and Beatrice Webb said: 'One [trade union regulation] stands out as practically universal, namely, the insistence on payments according to the same definite standard, uniform in its application.' And Hugh Clegg describes how during the period between the wars, 'many industries came to have a single national rate of pay for all areas . . . it came to be accepted more and more widely that an industry pay structure should be the ultimate objective of unions and employers in every industry' (both quotes cited by David Metcalf in 'Unions and the distribution of earnings', *British Journal of Industrial Relations*, July 1982, pp. 163–9).

Since the last war, two developments have made it easier for the unions to achieve this objective. The first is the growth of the public sector. Although less than half the workforce is employed in the public sector, it is very highly unionized. The only regional differential built into most public sector pay structures is a London weighting allowance. Otherwise the basic rate paid to, say, a hospital porter or a primary school teacher does not vary from Glasgow to Guildford — whatever the variations in the local labour supply. Earnings may vary, but that usually reflects cunning arrangements in overtime, designed to build back into the pay structure some of the flexibility removed by national wage agreements.

The other post-war development which has probably contributed to uniformity in pay rates has been the spread in private industry of local or company collective agreements, rather than national agreements between union and employers' organization. While on the face of it this has increased the diversity and complexity of bargaining in the private sector, and particularly in manufacturing, it has also brought pay back under the more direct control of employers and shop stewards in an individual firm or plant. In the early 1960s, bargaining between employers' organizations and union national executives tended to produce a settlement which then became a jumping off point for a mass of piecemeal agreements on the shop floor.

The growth of bargaining between individual employers and shop stewards has probably increased the exchange of information between shop stewards in different plants in the same firm, or the same industry. One of the most important influences on the mind of any union negotiator is comparability — what other groups are being paid for similar work.

An interesting study by Bill Daniel ('Influences on the level of wage settlements' in Frank Blackaby, ed., *The Future of Pay Bargaining*, Heinemann, 1980) found that the ability of employers to pay according to their financial circumstances seemed to have little influence on the formal increase in pay which was agreed. Comparability and compensation for the cost of living mattered much more. Also, union bargaining power was more likely to be used to protect members from getting too low an increase compared with the cost of living and the increases won by other groups of workers, than to take advantage of employers who were financially successful.

At this point, it is worth pausing for a moment to take stock. Some of the forces which help to determine what a worker is paid visibly reflect the forces of the market. For instance, higher education is still a relatively rare and valuable skill. But there are many ways in which the workings of the market are muted or frustrated: by discrimination against black workers or women, by the difficulty that older workers have in changing jobs, and by trade unions whose pressure to equalize pay runs directly counter to regional differences in the labour market (the supply of jobs) and the financial success or failure of employers (the demand for workers).

At the end of the day, it is hard to believe that the forces of the market do not have some impact on pay. As Sir Henry Phelps Brown points out in his book on the subject (*The Inequality of Pay*, Oxford University Press, 1977), the way in which different types of occupation are ranked according to pay differs very little between societies with such different social orders as the Western economies, the Soviet bloc, China and Cuba. It is easier to explain these similarities in terms of the play of market forces than by the influence of custom, convention or status.

And the two main changes in pay differentials in the course of time are easier to explain in terms of shifts of supply and demand than in terms of changing status or convention. The rise in the differential for skilled manual labour over unskilled which took place in the early stages of the industrial revolutions both in the West and in Stalin's Russia would be the logical consequence of a growth in demand; and the decline in the skill differential more recently – in both societies – suggests an increase in supply, and perhaps technological changes which have reduced the need for skill. In both Western economies and the Soviet bloc, there has been a decline in the pay of lower clerical grades relative to that of manual workers which might be a reflection of the extension of education for teenagers.

But while these slow changes in broad patterns of pay may reflect the force of the market, what happens at the level of the individual firm is more complicated and less rational. Differentials are sticky, supported by custom, convention and comparability. Employers rarely cut pay – even real pay, even relative pay. Instead, jobs for which there is declining demand tend to attract fewer new recruits, to have a middle aged (and therefore, since pay structures reward work experience) relatively well-paid workforce, and to offer declining opportunities for overtime and other ways of boosting basic pay.

Jobs which find it hard to attract enough recruits may have a relatively young (and therefore badly paid) workforce, most of whom will move on to better paid occupations in their late teens or early twenties. In the long run, pay may adjust to reflect supply and demand: but the availability of jobs will change faster.

Once one looks closely at pay, one has a sense of some huge structure, made up of a mass of little compartments which are connected by links which wobble from time to time but remain roughly in place. The broad distribution of earnings has hardly changed in a century: the best and the worst paid 10 per cent of male manual workers in 1886 earned almost precisely the same percentage of median male manual earnings as they did in 1981. Between some occupations, differentials have remained staggeringly constant. A famous study of craftsmen and labourers in the building industry showed the pay differential holding broadly constant at 3 to 2 for five centuries — from 1412 to 1914. Within the structure, individuals may travel from one compartment to another: a man who appears in the lowest paid tenth of male manual workers in one year seems to have only a one in five chance of staying there for five years in a row ('How individual people's earnings change', Department of Employment Gazette, January 1977, pages 19–24).

But from year to year, the structure moves up. Money earnings have been rising faster with every decade since the Second World War. And it is to the efforts of governments to restrain them that I know want to turn.

Employers have been concerned about the pace at which pay increased for a long time. But governments have become more concerned since the Second World War. There are perhaps two reasons for this. First, as the state has become a larger employer, it has inevitably become embroiled in pay negotiations. And second, as inflation gathered pace in the late 1960s and 1970s, it was obvious that increases in pay were often the immediate cause of rising prices.

So we saw a succession of attempts to control directly the rate at which money rates of pay were allowed to rise. We saw statutory policies and non-statutory policies, policies negotiated with the trade unions and policies introduced in the teeth of opposition from the unions, policies accompanied by price controls and policies with no price controls. There were pay freezes, percentage norms, flat rate norms, and combinations of percentage and flat rate limits. There were policies with boards to police them and policies without, policies with productivity clauses, and with special arrangements for the low paid. All the evidence suggests that not only did they fail, almost without exception, to reduce the rate of pay rises permanently: they also left the pay structure more complicated and riddled with fringe benefits, and they did very little for the low paid.

While they were in place, the on—off pay policies of the post-war period almost always slowed down the rate at which wages were rising. But the saga was almost always the same. The initial policy was tightly and simply drawn. People like simple policies: most people feel it is fairer for everyone to get nothing than for everyone to get, say, 5 per cent. Then the policy's very simplicity begins to destroy it. Some people have just had a pay rise and are quite happy: others were just about to negotiate one, and are furious. Some firms have negotiated new manning arrangements with their workers and need to sweeten the deal. Some want to promote, or to staff a new shop, or to improve pension rights. Once a pay policy tries to cope with all these eventualities it is doomed: it simply becomes too complicated to police. And the evidence suggests that in the months after it breaks down, the subsequent pay explosion may carry the rate of wage increases back to where it would have been had the pay policy never existed.

Nor have pay policies been much more successful at improving the plight of the low paid, a goal which has often been incorporated in them. Raising low pay is not a very constructive way of tackling family poverty, anyway: only one in five of the worst paid workers are in the poorest households, because most of them are married women, providing a second income. But for most of the six years between 1973 and 1979, pay policies intended to raise the relative pay of the poorest were in effect. At the end of the six years, there had been hardly any compression in the distribution of earnings between the best paid ten per cent of workers and the worst paid. Indeed those manual workers covered by Wages Council agreements (they tend to be the poorest paid) actually lost ground relative to all manual workers.

So the record of incomes policy is depressing. Probably the most lasting legacies of the 1960s and 1970s experiments have been a growth in trade union membership and a spread of fringe benefits, such as company cars and private health insurance, which were rarely included in the policies. Looking back, there was really only one policy which might arguably have been included as a success: and it was the first stage of the Labour government's policy in 1975. At that time, unemployment was rising and output stagnant. Unlike other periods of policy, the labour market was actually working in the same direction as pay restraint, rather than against it.

But given the generally patchy record, it is odd that governments persisted as long as they did. Why did they do it?

The short answer is the reply Gulbenkian is supposed to have made to the person who asked him about old age: 'It's better than the alternative.' Incomes policy is at least known to offer a short-term respite from wage inflation − enough, perhaps, for a government to fight an election. But curbing demand, a policy tested virtually to destruction in the early 1980s, patently involves massive costs in terms of the permanent destruction of human and physical capacity, and lost production, for only limited gains. [7] Nor is it clear that those gains will be any more lasting than the gains from incomes policy. The reasons are understandable enough. As we saw in the first half of this chapter, excessively high wage rates tend to be reflected in fewer new jobs: school leavers may be out of work, but those who already have jobs − and go to union meetings − are much less likely to become unemployed.

Incomes policy offers a government some hope − however temporary, however slender − that it will be able to curb the ability of the more powerful groups already in employment to negotiate higher pay at the expense of those who do not have jobs, and who will otherwise find it harder to get work. It ought to be a way of sharing out a reduction in the rate of growth of real incomes − and of controlling by consent the power of organized labour, which cannot yet be controlled by law.

As long as there is no neat economic explanation for short-term changes in money wages − and no-one has come up with one yet — it will be reasonable to assume that social and political forces may influence the course of pay, in the short run, more strongly than the state of the labour market. If workers look at what other groups of workers are earning (instead of at the prospects for demand for the product they make), if they have a concept of a 'going rate' linked, perhaps, to the figure for last year's rise in the cost of living, then they may be quite insensitive to the state of the job market in framing pay claims. In that case, it may be reasonable for governments to look for ways to change the social and political framework at the same time as they try to create an economic climate in which pay demands are likely to be moderated. Incomes policies have always performed worst when accompanied by rapid fiscal expansion.

Whether incomes policy is still a serious political possibility is more doubtful. The TUC made it clear at their conference in the autumn of 1982 that they would not discuss incomes policy with a Labour government. (With nice irony, the Confederation of British Industry a few weeks earlier had called for permanent pay restraint.) The TUC subsequently agreed to work out with a Labour administration a pay policy without a norm for pay. But the political party which has become a veritable haven for ingenious pay policies is the SDP. It has become particularly enthralled by two rather different schemes which Roy Jenkins described as 'exciting and novel'.

One, invented by Professor Richard Layard, is for an inflation tax. The government would set a norm for the permitted growth in hourly earnings, and a firm which paid more than this would incur a tax liability proportionate to the excess payment. The tax would be on firms, not workers; and would give employers a strong incentive to resist pay increases. It could be introduced without any agreement with the unions, and without any panoply of boards to police or enforce it.

The other scheme admired by the SDP was devised by Professor James Meade. It provides for a disputed pay settlement to be put to an arbitration court which has to decide the case solely on the grounds of which award will maximize employment. Acceptance of the arbitration decision is essentially voluntary.

There are drawbacks to both these schemes. Just to take

41

two, the Meade plan imposes on negotiators the formidable task of measuring the elasticity of demand for labour covered by a particular pay bargain. That might be hunky-dory for labour economists, who would suddenly find a vast increase in demand for their services, but not much help to workers or employers. The Layard scheme's main weakness is arguably that the brunt of the pressure will fall on firms in the private sector which are in competitive markets, either at home or − more probably − internationally. It is hard to see what impact the scheme would have in, say, health service disputes. And yet this is precisely the kind of dispute which is hardest to resolve: where a union or group of unions exercise an effective monopoly on the supply of a vital public service.

All governments are forced to have some view of the pay of their own employees, even if they are not prepared to go further than setting out the total increase in spending for which they are prepared to allow. Leaving public sector pay to the market place is out of the question. Not only is the public sector almost completely unionized: many of its services (hospitals, telephones, sewage) are effective monopolies. And many of its workers (local authority planning officers, soldiers, university lecturers) are in jobs for which there is no clear equivalent in the private sector.

In setting pay rates for its employees, the state has been torn between a desire to show a good example − or to restrain public expenditure − by setting rates low; a desire to try to evolve some system of comparability, which would allow public sector pay rates to be set automatically, by reference to some broadly comparable group of private sector workers; and a need to avoid politically damaging conflict. Because so many public sector workers are monopoly providers of services to the public, a strike over pay by hospital workers or staff in offices of the Department of Health and Social Security has a much more direct impact than a strike by a group of employees in ICI or the textile industry.

So governments always need − and have never yet managed to evolve − a satisfactory way of fixing pay for their own employees. The report by Sir John Megaw on a new system for determining civil service pay, published in the summer of 1982, may provide a partial solution: it recommended that the governing principle should be 'that the Government as an employer pays civil servants enough to recruit, retain and motivate them to perform efficiently the duties required of them at an appropriate level of competence'.

Such a system would almost certainly be easier to work within the framework of an incomes policy which covered the whole workforce, private sector as well as public. Its guiding principle would be the most hopeful one on which an incomes policy could be based. For any attempt to regulate pay needs to work *with* the forces of the labour market, rather than against them. Governments have rarely in the past made it a major object of policy to break down rigidities in the job market, by making the housing market more flexible, for instance, or by encouraging people to retrain for a different career in mid-life.

Incomes policies have not usually given much importance to the availability of labour for particular occupations. If there are masses of unemployed hospital porters but a severe shortage of nurses, it makes little economic sense to award the same increase to both groups. Nor does it make much sense to ignore the divergent pressures of regional jobs markets, and pay someone in Sunderland precisely the same rate for an unskilled job as someone in Croydon. But then 'economic sense' does not have much to do with principles of comparability, or going rates, or the other social conventions which dominate pay negotiations.

Questions

[1] Policies towards labour market imperfections

If pay, as the price of labour, were solely influenced by the forces of supply and demand, then rates of pay for different jobs would rise and fall in relative terms. These changes in relative prices act as signals to participants in the labour market and trigger movements of human resources between different industries. In this way a market system is presumed to allocate resources efficiently between competing uses.

Observed more closely, as in this chapter, there is evidence suggesting that the market system does not operate as efficiently as might be desired. In this situation you are involved in a classic example of the method of economics. Economic theory builds up a model of the labour market which assumes that the market operates perfectly. This yields certain predictions about rates of pay and levels of employment in particular industries. We then observe that our predictions are not fully confirmed by evidence around us. There are imperfections in the market system which prevent it from operating as predicted.

That does not necessarily mean the model is useless. It may simply describe an ideal world − in which wages would adjust to even out the distribution of unemployment. The more earnings respond sensitively and quickly to changes in the supply and demand for labour, the lower unemployment will be and the more evenly it will be shared throughout the country. The imperfections may simply point the government in the direction of policy measures, designed to allow the market system to operate as it should.

If the market is to work perfectly then certain well-known conditions have to apply:

a All units of the commodity (in this case labour) must be homogeneous (i.e. one unit exactly like another).

b No seller in the market can have monopoly power and no buyer the power of monopsony.

c There should be perfect knowledge available to all participants in the market − in this case concerning employment opportunities and rates of pay and conditions of work.

d There must be perfect mobility of the factors of production between alternative uses.

i *The chapter has thus far clearly shown how these conditions are not met. Now put yourself in the position of the Secretary of State for Employment in a government which believes that the economy will operate in everyone's best interests if market forces are allowed to operate as near perfectly as possible. Write your contribution to the Queen's Speech for the Opening of Parliament, outlining the practical measures which could be introduced to ensure that conditions a–d operate.*

ii   *You can measure your findings against the policy approach of the Department of Employment – obtain copies of 'Employment News', * the department's monthly newsletter, for the period 1979–83 and see what policy approaches Jim Prior and Norman Tebbitt emphasized in this period.*

[2]   Marginal productivity theory

Classical economic theory predicts that labour is rewarded in return for productivity. Profit maximizing firms hire labour to exploit the difference between the cost of employing labour and the revenue yielded by selling the product of labour. The greater the revenue product of labour, the greater the wage the employer is prepared to pay. Complete the following table where the revenue product is derived by multiplying the physical product by the price for which the product is sold – in this case taken to be £5 per unit.

Number of workers	Total product (units)	Average product	Marginal product	Average revenue product (£)	Marginal revenue product (£)
1	8				
2	24				
3	54				
4	82				
5	95				
6	100				
7	100				
8	96				

i   *What economic hypothesis is substantiated by the fact that in this case Marginal Product rises as the number of workers increases but eventually falls?*

ii   *What is the implication about market structure in which the firm operates if it can be assumed to sell any level of output for £5 per unit?*

* 'Employment News' is freely available. Write to the Department of Employment, Orphanage Road, Watford WD1 1PJ.

iii Construct a graph of the average revenue product and
    marginal revenue product figures – revenue product in
    money terms will be on the vertical axis and units of labour
    on the horizontal.

The profit maximizing firm will increase its labour employment providing that the addition to total cost of hiring the last
unit of labour is less than the additional revenue which accrues
to the firm when it sells the output resulting from that unit of
labour. The supply of labour to one firm is such that it can
obtain as many workers as it wishes, providing that it pays the
ruling wage rate.

iv How many workers will the firm employ when the wage
    rate is:
    a £80
    b £60
    Given that the wage rate is the price of labour, then the
    MRP curve tells us how much labour the firm will demand
    at each price (wage rate) – this is the function performed by
    any demand curve, so the MRP curve is referred to as the
    individual firm's demand for labour curve.

v Now assume that total product at all levels of employment
   is increased by 25%; calculate the revised MRP with the
   price for the product remaining at £5 per unit. Construct the
   revised MRP curve on your original graph – what level of
   employment will now result at a wage rate of £80?

vi Now read again the quoted findings of Derek Robinson's
    report (page 31). Are there any possible explanations for
    this apparent refutation of classical wage determination
    theory?

[3] Non-pecuniary benefits

'The curfew tolls the knell of parting day,
 The lowing herd wind slowly o'er the lea,
 The ploughman homeward plods his weary way,
 And leaves the world to darkness and to me.'
        Thomas Gray (1716–71), 'Elegy Written in a Country
                                            Churchyard'

Thomas Gray's lines which evoke dreams of bucolic tranquillity are a reminder that some people may choose to stay in lowly paid occupations because they feel compensated by factors other than their wages. No doubt the homeward journey from the fields is still somewhat less demanding than the 5.17 from Victoria and this may affect agricultural workers' perception of their living standards.

i *In what other occupations do you feel that people may frequently start a statement about their work with:*

   'The money's not that good but . . .'

ii *What other private benefits would you include in measuring the return on a job to an individual?*

[4] Education and pay

If it is general knowledge that every year spent in education beyond the age of 14 usually increases pay, then this must obviously influence the demand for further and higher education. It is possible to see the private demand for education as being an exercise in rational calculus where the individual's decision to 'stay on', 'go on' or 'go back' includes:

the increase in lifetime earnings as a consequence of increased education
less
the loss of income during the period of education
and
the cost of obtaining funds − which may/may not be zero even when grants are available.

This would yield a marginal net benefit concept which is presumably discounted by a subjective 'rate of time preference' − the rate at which the individual prefers present over future income when both are available.

A number of points need careful thought in this area:

i *How aware are people of their future earnings profile? If you have chosen a career do you know how much you will earn in 5 years' time with and without further education? What about 15 years' time?*

ii   Which factors did you consider to be relevant in making the decision to demand a further course of education?

iii   There is a shortage of places in higher education for 18-year-old school-leavers. Assuming the government wishes to alleviate this excess demand condition but does not wish to incur the costs associated with increasing the supply of places, how might it effect a policy to reduce the demand for education beyond the age of 16?

iv   In a market situation excess demand operates to raise the price. What is the effect of excess demand for university entrance?

v   Figure 6 shows a demand curve for education; the quantity axis is labelled as 'time units of education' but the vertical (price) axis is blank. In order to label this axis, explain what the price is that the private consumer has to pay for education. It will help if you consider, as the chapter points out, that education is a capital (investment) good.

Figure 6   An individual's demand for education

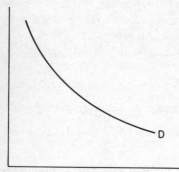

Time units of education

[5]   The economics of sex discrimination*

Assume:

a   There are equal numbers of men and women in the labour market.

_____

* This same analysis can be employed to observe the beneficial effect of the eradication of racial discrimination.

48

b Discrimination in the labour market in favour of men has produced a situation where women are excluded from employment in two industries with the result that female unemployment is concentrated in one industry.

c The three industries are ones in which the usual condition that male and female factor inputs are imperfect substitutes does not apply, so at any given wage level the employers will be just as willing to employ men as women.

Figure 7 shows how discrimination concentrates the female workforce into one industry. Figures 8 and 9 show the male workforce is divided equally between industries B and C.

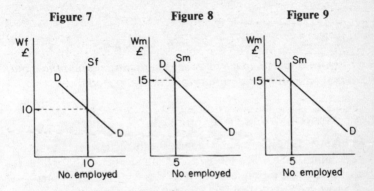

i *What is the total income earned by the female workforce?*

ii *What is the total income earned by the male workforce?*

iii *What, therefore, is the total income earned by the workforce?*

Figure 10 (p. 50) is the position where sex discrimination in the labour market has been removed totally. The demand curve for labour is now, for the purposes of this analysis, the horizontal sum of the three individual demand curves for the three industries. The supply curve is the joint supply of male and female labour.

iv *What now is the total income of the workforce?*

'Liberation of women, aside from being desirable and equitable for its own sake, provides also an enhancement of

Figure 10

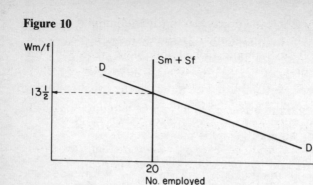

economic well-being through more efficient use of economic resources.'

Paul A. Samuelson, *Economics*, Xth edition, page 794

v By what means can men be seen to have benefited from the erosion of sex discrimination in the labour market?

[6] Wages, productivity and natural wastage

In Figure 11 the Marginal Revenue Product curve of labour in a particular firm has been shown as the firm's demand for labour curve. A trade union has negotiated a national wage increase (shown as a shift of W to W¹) which the firm is forced to accept in the short-run given the union's monopoly power in the supply of labour. As a result of the wage increase, the profit maximizing firm reduces its demand for labour by a–b workers.

Figure 11

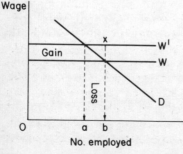

As it already employs Ob workers the model implies that the firm carries out a programme of redundancies. To avoid the expense and industrial unrest which this might create the firm may settle for a period of 'natural wastage' until the new desired level of labour Oa is reached.

i   What is natural wastage? Why might it involve 'greedy workers keeping young people out of employment'?

ii   In the light of your answer in (i), what is the significance of the two areas on the figure marked 'loss' and 'gain'?

iii   Unions can avoid this 'wages versus employment' syndrome by imposing 'agreed manning levels' on the firm so that position x is achieved: Ob employment at W^1 wage rate. What do you understand by agreed manning levels? Can you quote a current example? What can we say about the behaviour of a firm which accepts both the wage increase and the manning level?

The chapter points out, however, that higher wages may induce productivity increases in the workforce.

iv   Amend the figure to show how a wage-induced productivity increase could make the position x one which the employer was quite happy to accept.

v   By what argument do you think it is possible that paying workers higher wages encourages them voluntarily to raise productivity?

[7]   A case for incomes policy?

In May 1979 when the Conservative government took office, unemployment stood at around 1.3 million. The government's prime economic objective became that of effecting a substantial reduction in the rate of price increases, a rate which at that time approximated 10% and which reached 22% by mid-1980.

By February 1983 the rate of price increases had been brought down to 5%, achieved essentially by a policy of restricting the rate of growth of expenditure through controls over public expenditure, high interest rates and control of the money supply. The deflationary pressure which this exerted upon the economy was partly the cause of a rapid rise in unemployment which reached $3\frac{1}{2}$ million in 1983.

i   *In the light of this what does it mean to say that one of the functions of incomes policy is 'to reduce the unemployment cost of fighting inflation'?*

ii   *Comment upon the view that restricting demand to fight inflation is politically more attractive than incomes policy because, whereas incomes policy reduces the rate of growth of everyone's real income, restricting demand hurts only a minority who are rendered unemployed.*

Further reading

The most thorough recent discussions of what determines pay are *The Inequality of Pay* by Sir Henry Phelps Brown (Oxford University Press, 1977) and the background paper by Richard Layard and his colleagues quoted in the text (see page 33). The Metcalf chapter in Prest and Coppock (*The UK Economy*, Weidenfeld & Nicolson, 1982) is also very readable. There is an interesting discussion of incomes policy (largely by the converted) in *Pay Policies for the Future*, edited by Derek Robinson and Ken Mayhew (Oxford University Press, 1983). *Employment Gazette* (published monthly by the Department of Employment, Tothill St, London SW1 and available from HMSO) is essential reading for anyone fascinated by labour markets. It costs £32.76 for 12 copies; there is no reduced rate for schools.

3 Unemployment – is it here to stay?

Have the jobs gone for ever? Most of us instinctively forecast by extrapolating: after a decade in which unemployment has risen in almost every year to the 'low millions' which were unthinkable in the early 1970s, it requires a mighty leap of imagination to believe that we will return to the days when unemployment was measured in hundreds of thousands.

This chapter sets out to look first at why unemployment has risen. It is easier to explain the recent past than the mid-1970s. Then it looks at the reasons for hoping that the trend will turn – and the reasons for being more pessimistic. Finally, it takes a more speculative look at whether we can adjust to a society where work is a privilege, rather than a right.

There is not much argument about the reasons for the dramatic leap in unemployment in the late 1970s and early 1980s. There has been a massive recession – first in Britain, and then in our other big trading partners. You can argue about why demand collapsed: was it the result of the tough monetary policies of governments anxious to bring inflation under control, or was it (as a monetarist might argue) the inevitable corollary of inflation itself? But the bulk of the rise in unemployment, in Britain and other countries, since the end of the 1970s is simply what happens when companies find they cannot sell their products and therefore cannot afford to employ the workers who make them.

The force of recession has been compounded by a fluke of demography. The years immediately after the Second World War saw – in most industrial countries – a baby boom. Those babies grew up and married and had children of their own in the mid-1960s. It was these babies – the children of the war-babies – who began to leave school in large numbers at the end of the 1970s. The numbers of young people aged between 16 and 24 grew by 9 per cent in Britain between

1977 and 1981, and will grow by another 3 per cent by 1986. This surge of youngsters onto the job market has coincided with a dip in the numbers of men reaching retirement age: the generation born during the First World War. So existing jobs are not falling vacant as fast as usual; and the economy is less able than usual to create new jobs. The result has been a particular concentration of unemployment among the luckless young. [1]

But there is still a mystery. Take a look at Figure 12, showing job vacancies notified to job centres measured against the rise in unemployment. If you cover up the unemployment figures and look simply at what has been happening to notified vacancies − once widely regarded as the most accurate indicator of the state of the job market − you might be forgiven for wondering what on earth all the fuss was about. While the numbers of unemployed have risen almost year by year, the number of notified vacancies has wavered round a fairly constant mean. Nor is this an exclusively British phenomenon. A collection of papers edited by Martin Neil Baily called *Workers, Jobs and Inflation* (Brookings Institution, Washington, DC, 1982) opens with an introduction by the editor who makes this observation: 'The unemployment figures are really the only ones that show chronic slack in the 1970s. Measures of labor turnover and help-wanted advertising suggest that, apart from 1975−6, the 1970s were a period of normal labour demand.'

Some change seems to have taken place in the labour market in the 1970s − not just in Britain, but in the US and perhaps in other industrial countries, too. Either employers changed the terms on which they were willing to take on workers or workers changed the terms on which they were willing to be employed. There are perhaps three front runners among possible explanations.

One is that the amount of money which people can get when they are not in work has gone up, relative to pay. There has by now been a vast amount of work on what are called 'replacement ratios': the ratio between the benefits an out-of-work person can receive and the after-tax wage they can expect to earn. In 1982 the government abolished the Earnings Related Supplement for which the newly unemployed qualified. It

Figure 12 Unemployment and vacancies: United Kingdom 1965–83

Three-month moving average: seasonally adjusted

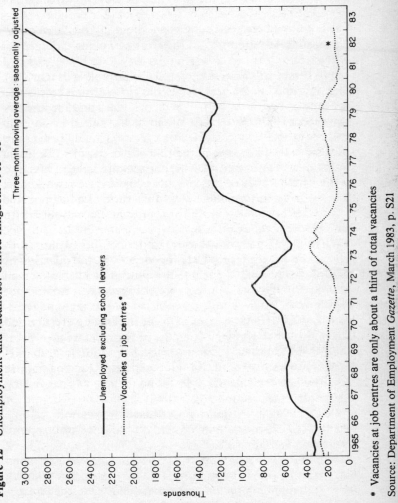

Unemployed excluding school leavers
Vacancies at job centres*

* Vacancies at job centres are only about a third of total vacancies

Source: Department of Employment *Gazette*, March 1983, p. S21

hoped eventually to tax unemployment benefit, precisely because it believed that the combined effect of taxation and benefit was to encourage some people to postpone looking for a job − and so to raise the total numbers unemployed at any given time.

There was almost certainly some grounds for their worry. The most up-to-date study of the effects of taxes and benefits on the decision to work was published by C. N. Morris and A. W. Dilnot of the Institute for Fiscal Studies in October 1982. It looked at the years from 1968 to 1978 and found that increases in direct taxation on people at work and the increasing generosity of the benefit system had resulted in a steady upward trend in replacement rates. In 1980 some 11 per cent of individuals could expect, in the first weeks out of work, to be getting over 90 per cent of what they would have received in work. And because of the way the benefit system worked, it made sense for many people − about a third of all individuals − who had been out of work for four weeks to wait for a fifth week before accepting a job.

What all this boils down to is that there probably are some people who take longer to look for a job − and so push up the unemployment total − because they do more or less as well on the dole. But the total numbers are not very large: they do not include more than a tiny fraction of the long-term unemployed; and the 1982 changes in the benefit and tax system will reduce them still further. There is, of course, a related point which it is harder for economists to analyse: there is a widespread suspicion that a lot of people are earning money illegally while drawing the dole − and thus, of course, raising their replacement ratios substantially. [2]

We all have our stories to prove that this is happening on a gigantic scale. I saw a note pinned on the door of a second-hand furniture shop saying 'Dear Fred, Gone to sign on. Back in ten minutes. Charlie'. But before one assumes that 'scrounging' explains away a large part of the rise in unemployment, there are a number of points to bear in mind. First, the assumption that the unemployed are out of work because they are dishonest and/or lazy always grows in periods of high unemployment. It did during the great depression between the wars. It is the way those of us with jobs try to reconcile ourselves to our own good fortune. In fact, the opportunities for working on the dole are much greater in periods of low unemployment — when the economy is running full-tilt — than in the midst of a major recession.

Second, it is a great deal easier to work on the dole in a big city — like London — than in a smaller town — like Scunthorpe. There are more opportunities, and less chance of being found out. But the serious pockets of unemployment tend by and large to be outside London, in medium-sized towns whose main companies have gone to the wall.

So a change in the relationship between what people can earn in work and out of it probably does not explain much of what happened in the labour market in the 1970s. A second front-runner as an explanation is that there was a change in the terms on which employers were willing to take on labour. There seems unquestionably to have been a rise in the cost of labour compared to its productivity. On the one hand, the indirect costs of employing labour have gone up: partly as a result of government policy (the UK National Insurance surcharge, for instance, which effectively operates as a payroll tax) and partly as a result of the spread of fringe benefits (occupational pensions, longer holidays, shorter working hours). On the other hand, there has been a measurable rise in real wages relative to the value of labour's output. [3]

This has been most obvious in Europe. Some work in the Common Market Commission's economic directorate looked at the gap between the real wages paid by companies in Europe, the USA and Japan and the wages which (judged by productivity and the terms of trade) they could afford to pay. The study found that in Europe, a large gap in favour of wages and against profits opened in the wake of the first oil shock in 1973. It did not continue to increase after 1975, but it did not close either.

There are good explanations for this gap which at once suggest themselves. The obvious one is the inflexibility of real pay. The rise in the oil price squeezed profits, but did not squeeze real wages to anything like the same extent; the recession years of the 1970s had the same effect. And why was pay so inflexible? Well, partly because it always had been (see chapter 2) and partly, perhaps, because the 1970s were a time of growing trade union membership and power. As chapter 2 suggests, the driving force behind pay increases in the private sector in the UK has come increasingly from companies with a lot of market power and not much sensitivity to labour market conditions.

There are two problems, though, with explanations of this sort. First, real wages seem to have behaved in Japan in very much the same way as they did in Europe – rocketing up in the wake of the oil shock, relative to what companies could 'afford', and then levelling off. But Japan did not suffer the long rise in unemployment which Europe experienced in the mid-1970s. Second, explanations of this sort work much better for the first half of the 1970s than for the second. Some work published in the *Midland Bank Review* (Economic Outlook, Autumn 1980, pages 1–8) looks at what happened to the 'real product wage' in the UK – basically, the total cost of a unit of labour to an employer in manufacturing, compared with value added per unit of output. From the mid-1960s to the late 1970s, there was a neat tendency for rising 'real product wages' to go together with falling employment. As labour became more and more expensive to the employer in real terms, there were fewer and fewer jobs. But in the late 1970s, the relationship became much harder to establish.

A third possible explanation is that the important change was not in what workers wanted to earn or what employers felt willing to pay them, but in the kind of jobs which the economy needed. Some fundamental change, so the argument runs, altered the kind of skills in demand in a way which the labour force could not deliver.

There is certainly evidence of an important shift in the kinds of jobs created by the economy since the late 1960s and early 1970s; and there are some elegant theories to explain why a structural change might have occurred – though marrying the two up is not always very easy. The most striking change has been the disappearance of large numbers of jobs in manufacturing. This process of 'de-industrialization' has happened in a lot of Western economies. In the UK, manufacturing jobs began to disappear in absolute numbers after 1966, and from that date to 1982 some 3 million manufacturing jobs have disappeared. Over the same period, $1\frac{1}{2}$ million new jobs were created in the service industries. By September 1982, services employed more than twice as many people as manufacturing. But the vanishing jobs have tended, by and large, to be full-time jobs for men; and the new jobs have tended, by and large, to be part-time jobs for women. Women now make up 43 per cent of the workforce, and one employee in five is a part-timer. [4]

There have been plenty of theories for the decline in manufacturing employment. Perhaps the most famous (Bacon and Eltis) argued that it was essentially the fault of the expanding public sector: public sector employees did not, by and large, produce goods or services which could be exported, but their pay bills added to the cost of the private sector, which included most exporting industries. A rather simpler version of this theory is put forward in the papers on de-industrialization from a conference on the subject held by the National Institute in 1978 (*De-industrialisation*, edited by Frank Blackaby, Heinemann, 1979). The decline of manufacturing employment is linked to the slow growth of manufacturing output and exports, which in turn is a manifestation of the familiar British problem of poor international competitiveness. Meanwhile service industry employment has grown partly because the state paid for a lot of it, and partly because few services are exportable enough to stand the test of foreign competition.

That makes a lot of sense: although the decline in competitiveness (like the fall in the relative size of manufacturing employment) has been around for three decades. But a number of theories suggest that there may have been a more recent, dramatic and international structural change in the demand for labour.

One of the most interesting versions, and one to which I return in the next chapter, has been put forward by Michael Beenstock (*The World Economy in Transition*, George Allen & Unwin, 1983). He argues that the balance of world economic power has been shifting from the industrial world to the Third World. The increase in output from the newly industrializing countries (NICs) depressed the prices of manufactured goods in the late 1960s and early 1970s and thus cut the return to capital in the OECD countries. Investment began to flow from the developed to the developing countries: quite logically, as capital flowed from Britain to the New World to finance economic expansion a century ago. But jobs, particularly jobs in low wage manufacturing, also disappeared in the developed countries.

A more familiar version of this theory of mismatch between employers' needs and workers' skills takes the rise in the price of oil in the early 1970s as the trauma which changed the structure of the job market. The price of one essential commodity − a commodity almost as widely used, as intrinsic in the mesh of costs and prices as labour itself − rose dramatically in relation to the prices of all other commodities. Moreover, it rose at a time when there was already considerable inflation in the world economy: and that inflation made it harder for workers and management to read the change in relative price signals which would usually have been the way in which the economy announced the need for structural change. But through the 1970s it became increasingly clear that industries which were big users of energy, or which relied for their marketability on cheap energy, were going to be much less profitable than industries in whose costs and sales energy played little part. Hence the collapse of steel, large American cars, shipbuilding, charter flights; and the growth of small Japanese cars, video games, private health care.

I find the second of these theories of structural change a more convincing explanation of the past decade than the first. The rise of the newly industrialized countries is certainly going to have an important effect on manufacturing employment in the West for many decades to come; but it is only very recently − in the late 1970s − that the NICS have come to account for a significant share of some categories of manufactured exports. On the other hand, the impact and scale of the oil price rise − of the two rises, in 1973−4 and again in 1975−6 − have generally been underestimated rather than exaggerated.

To sum up the story so far, there are three possible explanations for the shift which seems to have taken place in the 1970s in the structure of the job market. It may have been that more workers found it in their financial interest to postpone taking a new job if they became unemployed; or it may have been that the cost to employers of labour rose very much faster than labour's productivity; or it may have been that the demand for labour changed in some way that caused shortages of some kinds of workers and large oversupply of others. Probably it was some combination of the three. But the net result was to raise by a large amount the unemployment rate at which the economy showed signs of operating near full capacity.

And that creates an impediment to dealing with the unemployment which the recession has caused. How important the impediment is depends on how much of the current unemployment you attribute to the structural changes which I have just been rehearsing (and monetarists would give them a lot of weight) and how much you attribute to shortage of demand. If you are in the first camp, you worry that a policy of expansion would quite quickly run up against constraints of capacity and that the result would be an early resurgence of inflation. [5] If you are in the second camp, you think that is ridiculous. You observe that in 1979, with unemployment at $1\frac{1}{4}$ million, it may have been reasonable to worry about whether capacity constraints had altered. But you point out that it is inconceivable that structural change accounts for the subsequent loss of over two million jobs. Anyway a bit more inflation is a small price to pay for dealing with the misery of over 3 million people out of work.

But the chances are that the impediment, real or exaggerated, will continue to influence government policy well into the 1980s: and not just in Britain. The length and severity of the recession will be determined much less by what the British government does than by the combined effect of the policies of the United States, West Germany, and the other major countries of the OECD. One of the great dilemmas for any middle-sized economy is whether to act alone: to expand in a world of contraction, risking balance of payments deficit, a weakening exchange rate, and so ultimately renewed inflation and high interest rates. To end a major world recession requires concerted policies by the giant economies, and of this there has been little sign.

That is the main reason for suspecting that high unemployment will continue through most of the 1980s. It is a much more important reason than the one which attracts more publicity — the impact of the new technology. It is one of the curiosities of intellectual fashion that while politicians in the 1960s worried that too little investment would prevent the creation of new jobs, today they worry about too much investment as a potential cause of unemployment.

There is, as it happens, precious little evidence of technological unemployment on a significant scale so far. The late 1970s were a time of disturbingly low investment. There were few signs of a fall in the demand for unskilled workers relative to skilled: no steady rise in productivity, no widening of the differential between the earnings of the skilled and unskilled. It may, of course, happen in the future that the revolution in electronics and telecommunications will reduce the overall number of jobs in the economy. If so, it will probably be because the new technology reduces the demand for unskilled labour relative to skilled labour, or changes the kinds of skills which the economy demands.

But it is much easier to see when new technology destroys a job than when it creates one. Every major technological change in the past has been heralded as likely to cause permanent job loss. In the 1960s there were endless jokes about people being replaced by computers. There were one or two well-publicized cases of large-scale redundancies as a direct and demonstrable effect of computerization − in mail-order companies, for instance. But it is hard now, in retrospect, to see the 1960s as a period of technologically induced unemployment. It is easy to guess which jobs will become vulnerable as a result of the latest technological change. It is very much harder to predict where new jobs will come from. But the new technology extends to small businesses facilities − for things like stock control and booking lists − which were once only available to very big firms. It ought to be possible for a small hotel to improve its occupancy rates, a small grocery store its stock control, a small building firm its billing system.

But it is not only in direct ways, by facilitating new enterprises, that technological change may create jobs. One of the hardest concepts to absorb is that new investment which raises productivity makes the country wealthier. If the installation of a word processor or mini-computer allows the same number of people to produce more than they were doing before, or allows fewer people to produce the same as was being produced before, the same goods or services are being made available more cheaply. That wealth may be shared out in a variety of ways: the workers may demand it all in higher pay as a reward for operating the new machines or the consumer may reap the benefit in lower prices, or the employer may make bigger profits, or the government's tax take may go up. The extra wealth may be spent on creating more jobs in Britain (by eating out more often for instance, or buying a Burberry) or it may be spent on creating jobs abroad (by buying a video recorder). But there is no way that a new investment can impoverish the community.

Self-evidently, new investment redistributes jobs: newspaper type may be set by 18-year-old girls, paid £7000 a year, instead of middle-aged men paid £20,000 a year. And the most interesting — and alarming — thing to anyone looking at the likely pattern of employment over the rest of the 1980s is that it is a lot easier to see where jobs for women will come from than jobs for men.

From the point of view of the employer, there are all sorts of good arguments for employing women part-timers than men full-timers. They are relatively cheap. It is not just that women generally earn less than men: part-timers qualify for fewer fringe benefits — holidays, sick pay, occupational pensions. They are more flexible — just think of the advantages to the Post Office of being able to employ part-timers to sort and deliver the mail, or to British Rail in using part-timers to drive commuter trains. They are less likely to join trade unions, and less likely to strike. And, more than men, they tell market researchers that they enjoy work. What more could an employer ask for?

Add to this the fact that we are more likely to see an expansion of employment in the service industries (which predominantly employ women) than in manufacturing (which predominantly employs men). As people become richer (and some of us, at least, will continue to become richer in the 1980s) they want to spend a rising proportion of their additional wealth on services: on education for their children and perhaps for themselves, on taking out private health insurance, on a more glamorous (or more frequent) holiday, on celebrating their wedding anniversary at Cartier's restaurant instead of Fred's cafe. [6]

They will want a better quality of service. And with most services, the only way to achieve better quality is by reducing productivity. That, of course, is very different to manufacturing, where improvements in quality may actually be more likely if production becomes more highly mechanized – and so may be linked to increases in productivity. But one of the main things that attracts people to private sector education is that their children will be taught in smaller classes than in the public sector; one of the things which makes people book into the London Clinic for their hernia operation is that they will be seen more quickly by a doctor; one of the things people expect when they eat at the Savoy Grill is at least three waiters cooling around them. So the chances are that as the demand for services rises, so will service employment.

But three, or perhaps four, million people, at least two-thirds of them men, may have to get used to life without employment. There are all kinds of ingenious theories about how we could make this more bearable. We ought, some argue, to encourage people to share their jobs, or to work part-time, to spread the existing supply of work among more people. We ought, say others, to change the way we think about work, so that it becomes less important as a way of defining people's status in the eyes of their fellow citizens. [7]

In a way, these ideas are simply ways of encouraging men to behave like married women. But the circumstances of most married women and most men are very different. There have been experiments with job sharing – mainly by women who want to continue working after they have children. Most part-timers are married women. They are willing – and this is the crucial point – to give up the income of a full-timer in exchange for a toehold in the job market. No employer has an incentive to split a job if the two halves will cost more than the whole; and for a man with a family, a part-time job may have precious little financial attraction compared with being on the dole.

It would be nice to believe that we could learn to regard work in a more flexible way: not just as what we get paid for, and not as the touchstone of our status. Half the human race does a great deal of work for nothing. To reply to the question, 'What do you do?' with 'I'm a housewife' may carry less social stigma than saying 'I'm unemployed' – but not much.

It is paid work which still defines our place in society. It is because unemployment deprives people of their social place that it hurts — not just because it deprives them of income. That is why tackling unemployment needs more than ingenious wheezes.

Questions

[1] Structure of population

i *Carefully read through the passage again (p. 54) and relate it to Figure 13 (p. 66). Now consider the following:*
  a *Approximately how many people aged 20 were there in mid-1980?*
  b *Approximately how many people were there aged 65?*

ii *At the end of the First World War (1919) the number of births increased suddenly. This should have produced a further 'baby boom' in the period 1936–40 but it did not occur. Can you suggest reasons for this?*

iii *The age structure of the population is currently affecting the labour market as outlined in the chapter. What other structural effects are likely to occur as the current age group of 10–20 year olds grows older?*

[2] Replacement ratios

'A very significant change that has occurred since the early 1960s when the natural rate of unemployment was half-a-million or so is the very large increase in the ratio of social security benefits to average earnings less tax. Whatever this ratio may be for the average worker, it has risen significantly: the unemployed now receive between one-third and a half more than they used to in the early 1960s relative to the net-of-tax earnings of those at work. It is, therefore, straightforward economic analysis that the cost of "searching" for

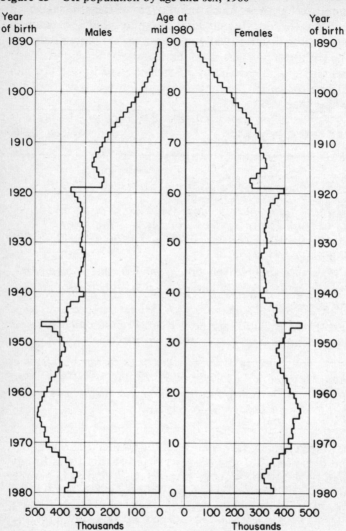

Figure 13   UK population by age and sex, 1980

Source: *Social Trends*, HMSO, 1982

better paid work, either by going on strike or by changing employers has been much reduced. No wonder then an extra million workers are searching for better paid work than in the 1950s and early 1960s, and that they are prepared to use the strike weapon even if it threatens the bankruptcy of their companies and the ending of their present jobs. They can afford to search for other work which will pay them the wages they seek.'

Walter Eltis, *Job Creation or Destruction?*, Institute of Economic Affairs, 1979

The replacement ratio can be expressed as:

$$\frac{\text{benefit paid per recipient}}{\substack{\text{post-tax male manual earnings,} \\ \text{full-time workers aged over 21}}} = \text{replacement ratio}$$

i   *If this expression yields a value of 1, what can you deduce about the two figures?*

ii   *What two approaches could be adopted to reduce the replacement ratio — which of them is likely to be politically most acceptable?*

Metcalf and Richardson* give the following data relating to replacement ratios:

	replacement ratio	*unemployment*
1964–5	.33	330,000
1973	.37	580,000

They then introduce the concept of the elasticity of unemployment duration. Like any elasticity measure this quantifies the extent to which one variable responds to a change in another causal factor. In this case we are looking at the extent to which people will choose to remain unemployed for longer as a result of the increase in the replacement ratio. Crudely we could write:

$$\frac{\text{\% change in unemployment}}{\text{\% change in replacement ratio}}$$

* In A. R. Prest and D. J. Coppock, *The UK Economy*, 9th edition, Weidenfeld & Nicolson, 1982, page 263.

The value for this is thought to be around +0.6 (that is a 10% rise in the replacement ratio would produce a 6% rise in unemployment).

iii   *What was the percentage increase in the replacement ratio between 1964–5 and 1973?*

iv   *What then was the percentage change in unemployment, caused by the increase in the replacement ratio during the same period?*

v   *The original level of unemployment was 330,000. Increase this by your percentage answer to (iv) and you have an approximation of how much unemployment rose due to the rise in the replacement ratio.*

Pursuing this analysis Metcalf and Richardson conclude:

Assuming such estimates are reliable, it is clear that the disincentive effects associated with more generous unemployment benefits account for only a modest fraction of the rise in unemployment.

vi   *In his book 'The British Economy' (Philip Allan, 1982) Professor Maurice Peston argues that the replacement ratio has fallen by some 8% since 1971. Using what Walter Eltis calls 'straightforward economic analysis', explain what should have happened to the level of unemployment.*

[3]   The tax on jobs

The National Insurance surcharge can be seen as a 'tax on jobs' being paid by the employer as a contribution per employee towards the cost of running the National Insurance scheme. If you employ somebody you not only have to pay the wage rate but also have to pay the government. The effect on the demand for labour can be shown in Figure 14.

Without the interference of government the interaction of supply and demand in the labour market yields an equilibrium wage rate of Ow and a level of employment of Oa. The employers' National Insurance charge is in effect an indirect tax

Figure 14

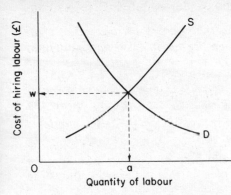

on the 'consumption' of labour. Governments introduce indirect taxes for two possible reasons:

a   to raise revenue – duty on alcohol; VAT
b   to put people off consuming the product – import tariffs

The cost to the employer of engaging Oa workers will not be Ow per worker but Ow + National Insurance charge. This will be true at all levels of employment. If the charge is levied as a percentage of the wage, then the higher the wage rate, the greater the tax. In the figure this will have the effect of shifting the supply curve vertically upwards, whilst it pivots on its base.

i   *Reproduce Figure 14; introduce the 'S + tax' curve and explain in your own words why the vertical distance between it and the original supply curve becomes greater as you move up the curve.*

ii   *Given that the supply curve in the model is the Marginal Cost curve of hiring extra labour and the demand curve is the Marginal Revenue Product derived from hiring extra units of labour, how will the profit maximizing firm react to the introduction of the National Insurance charge?*

iii   *For the introduction of a tax on labour to have no effect upon employment levels, the demand curve for labour has to assume a unique shape. Show this on your diagram – what does it say about the demand for labour and why would this be seen as very unusual if not impossible?*

iv *This analysis concludes that there is a strong case for the abolition of the employers' National Insurance surcharge. Now suppose a government went even further, and abolished employers' contributions to the National Insurance scheme altogether. Instead, firms might be told to subscribe to a private system of pension schemes, health care, etc. What difference would it make if the employer made a regular payment per employee every month to the Prudential and BUPA instead of to the Department of Health and Social Security?*

[4] Female economic activity

Examine Tables 3 and 4 (pp. 71–3).

i *Carefully explain why the economic activity rate of women in the UK has risen substantially in the past two decades.*

ii *What detailed arguments can be drawn from these two tables to show that it is very unlikely that increased female economic activity has 'caused' male unemployment?*

iii *Given that an increase in the female activity rate is in effect an increase in the supply of labour available, what might it have influenced? Some male trade unionists argue that an increase in women workers holds down wages. Is that fair?*

[5] The aggregate supply curve

The two 'camps' mentioned here reflect a crucial debate in current economic policy. As is often the case, crucial debate in economics can be examined using simple techniques in the subject.

The question embracing the controversy is 'what happens to the economy if the government embarks upon a policy of expansion?' Expansion means to raise the level of nominal income or what Samuel Brittan describes as 'Money GDP' (see pp. 18–19). It can be achieved through either monetary or

Table 3 UK employees in employment by industry[1] (thousands)

	1961	1966	1971	1976	1979	1980		
						Males	Females	All
Agriculture, forestry, and fishing	710	580	432	393	367	277	93	370
Mining and quarrying	727	570	396	348	346	328	17	344
Manufacturing								
Food, drink, and tobacco	793	797	770	714	698	409	271	681
Chemicals, coal and petroleum products	499	495	482	460	482	344	126	470
Metal manufacture	643	627	557	469	444	355	47	401
Engineering and allied industries	3,654	3,778	3,615	3,269	3,270	2,442	680	3,121
Textiles, leather and clothing	1,444	1,319	1,124	935	898	330	483	813
Rest of manufacturing	1,508	1,571	1,511	1,399	1,386	946	376	1,322
Total manufacturing	8,540	8,587	8,058	7,246	7,176	4,827	1,981	6,808
Construction	1,485	1,648	1,262	1,309	1,292	1,156	109	1,265
Gas, electricity and water	389	432	377	353	346	277	69	347
Services								
Transport and communication	1,678	1,622	1,568	1,475	1,494	1,211	289	1,500
Distributive trades	2,767	2,920	2,610	2,723	2,826	1,248	1,542	2,790
Insurance, banking and finance	684	818	976	1,103	1,233	584	674	1,258
Professional and scientific services	2,124	2,591	2,989	3,655	3,729	1,172	2,545	3,717
Miscellaneous services	1,819	2,066	1,946	2,299	2,493	1,060	1,459	2,519
Public administration	1,311	1,424	1,509	1,631	1,619	971	625	1,596
Total services	10,382	11,441	11,597	12,886	13,394	6,246	7,133	13,379
All industries and services	22,233	23,257	22,122	22,543[2]	22,920	13,110	9,401	22,511

[1] As at June each year. [2] In 1976 8,600 employees were not allocated to individual industry-groups, but are included in the total.

Source: *Social Trends*, HMSO, 1982

Table 4 Economic activity rates[1] by age and sex, Great Britain (%)

		15–19[2]	20–24	25–44	45–59/64[3]	60/65+[4]	All ages
Married females							
Estimates[5]	1961	41.0	41.3	33.1	32.6	7.3	29.7
	1966	43.6	43.5	41.8	46.3	12.1	38.1
	1971	41.6	45.7	46.4	53.4	14.2	42.2
	1977	54.7	59.0	59.1	61.9	12.3	50.4
	1979	50.9	57.8	58.7	61.0	10.1	49.6
Projections[6]	1980	51.1	57.7	58.6	61.4	9.8	49.3
	1981	50.7	57.6	58.0	61.8	9.3	48.8
	1984	50.5	57.6	58.8	64.1	8.9	49.5
	1986	50.9	57.7	59.3	65.0	8.0	49.9
Non-married females							
Estimates[5]	1961	73.2	89.4	84.8	70.5	12.1	50.6
	1966	68.4	86.7	84.2	72.8	12.9	49.2
	1971	57.2	81.2	80.4	73.4	11.0	43.7
	1977	62.7	78.0	78.9	71.8	7.3	42.1
	1979	65.9	78.1	78.4	70.9	5.3	42.8
Projections[6]	1980	65.6	78.9	78.2	70.8	4.8	42.9
	1981	65.4	79.4	78.1	70.7	4.4	43.1
	1984	65.1	80.2	77.8	70.7	4.0	43.6
	1986	64.8	80.1	77.7	70.5	3.6	43.6
All females							
Estimates[5]	1961	71.1	61.8	40.3	41.4	10.0	37.3
	1966	66.5	61.6	47.3	52.0	12.6	42.2

	Col1	Col2	Col3	Col4	Col5	Col6
1971	55.9	60.1	50.6	57.4	12.4	42.7
1977	62.0	67.7	61.9	63.8	9.5	47.4
1979	64.8	67.9	61.8	62.9	7.4	47.0
Projections[6]						
1980	64.5	68.5	61.7	63.2	6.9	46.9
1981	64.2	68.9	61.4	63.6	6.5	46.6
1984	63.8	69.2	62.3	65.4	6.1	47.2
1986	63.6	69.1	62.8	66.1	5.5	47.4
All males Estimates[5]						
1961	74.6	91.9	98.5	96.8	25.0	86.0
1966	70.6	92.6	98.2	95.1	23.5	84.0
1971	60.9	89.9	97.9	94.5	19.4	81.4
1977	67.9	89.0	97.8	92.7	13.4	79.8
1979	70.7	88.3	97.4	91.2	10.2	78.6
Projections[6]						
1980	70.7	88.4	97.2	89.8	8.9	77.8
1981	70.9	38.9	97.0	88.4	8.0	77.3
1984	71.2	89.7	96.9	86.1	7.1	77.2
1986	71.3	90.0	97.2	85.9	7.2	77.1

[1] Excluding students in full-time education.

[2] From 1973 15 year olds are excluded as a result of the raising of the school-leaving age. Figures 1977 therefore relate to 16–19 year olds.

[3] 45–59 for females, 45–64 for males.

[4] 60+ for females, 65+ for males.

[5] Estimates for 1961–71 are taken directly from the Census of Population. Estimates for 1977–79 are based on the EC Labour Force Surveys.

[6] Projections are based on estimates from the 1979 EC Labour Force Survey.

Source: *Social Trends*, HMSO, 1982.

fiscal means, or a combination of both. However, nominal income (the Y of economics textbooks) has two components — it is essentially

real output × the price level

A policy designed to raise nominal income will, therefore, either raise real output (Q) or raise the price level (p) or raise both in some order, or, possibly, raise one substantially but reduce the other. The problem is to know in advance what the price and output changes are likely to be.

To explore price and output effects of raising the level of demand, economics employs supply and demand analysis. To resolve the debate between the committed monetarist and the sceptical Keynesian, we employ the same analysis here.

Figure 15 shows an Aggregate Demand curve for an economy. The shift in the curve reflects the policy of expansion.*

Figure 15

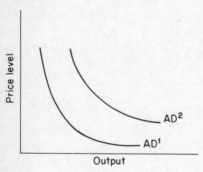

To 'know' what effect this shift in the demand curve will have upon price and output and hence the composition of Money GDP, you need a supply curve for the economy.

i   *It is possible that the supply curve could have a shape which predicts that all the expansion of nominal income comes through an increase in output. What shape supply curve will produce this effect?*

* For a detailed discussion of the shape of the AD curve and for a more thorough assessment of this debate, see *Modern Economic Analysis 2*, D. H. Gowland (ed.), Butterworth, 1982.

*ii It is equally possible that the effect of expansion will be
purely to raise the price level. What shape supply curve will
produce this effect?*

Increases in real output will be reflected in reductions of unemployment. Expanding the economy from a given level of
output/unemployment will result in either price increases or
reductions in unemployment, given the supply curves above.
How the economy performs in this 'inflation/unemployment
trade-off' is too often analysed through the so-called Phillips
curve. To know the nature of the Phillips curve trade-off one
must, logically, know the shape of the AS curve. Given that it
can assume a variety of possible shapes, the Phillips curve has
no reliable predictive power.

*iii What factors are likely to determine the ease with which
the economy can increase real output when demand expands?*

[6] Service industries — the employment possibility

This analysis employs a simple, but often under-utilized, concept in economics. Income elasticity of demand measures the
response of demand for a product to a change in the level of
income:

$$\frac{\% \text{ change in quantity demanded}}{\% \text{ change in GDP}}$$

It is this concept which is at the basis of the argument here.

Say that, as income rises, people in a particular economy
change their expenditure pattern in the following way: they
reduce their demand for domestic manufactured products
such as cars (possibly because of a preference for imported
vehicles) but increase their demand in the catering industries
(more meals out, 'bargain break' weekends). It might be
reasonable to place the following values to income elasticity of
demand:

hotel catering services   = 1.0
domestically produced cars = −0.1

*i Given a 10% increase in GDP, what are we claiming would
happen to the demand for the two products?*

It also seems a reasonable assertion that the hotel-catering industry is more labour intensive in its production methods than the motor industry as illustrated in these 'hypothetical' figures:

	employment	output	output per employee
Catering	1,000,000	£1,750m	
Vehicle manufacture	400,000	£4,000m	

For the sake of simplicity we will assume that the labour: output ratios remain constant at all levels of output.

ii   *If demand in the domestic car industry drops by 1%, what reduction is this in value terms and what effect does it have on employment?*

iii   *If demand rises in the catering industries by 10%, what increase in output is this in value terms and what effect does it have on employment?*

iv   *What is the net effect on employment in the economy?*

[7]   The work ethic

Changing the way a society thinks about work may be a crucial issue which young people will have to face. The work ethic is part of our social value system: true participation in society comes only through work. It can be argued that religions operate to confirm in the people the belief that to be without work is somehow 'sinful':

'For even when we were with you, this we commanded you,
 that if any would not work, neither should he eat,
 For we hear that there are some which would walk among you
 disorderly, working not at all, but are busy-bodies.'

Second Epistle of Paul the Apostle
to the Thessalonians 3:10

'To learne and labour to get mine own living,
and to do my duty in that state of life, unto which
it shall please God to call me.'

Catechism of the Book of Common Prayer

i   *How widespread are such beliefs? Do they affect your own
thinking about work? Are such exhortations to work true of
all religions?*

ii *If you find the notion that established religions operate to
promote the work ethic an irrelevancy, try an alternative
line of thought. How do you answer the following questions:*
'What do you do?'
'What do you want to do when you leave school?'
'What are you doing with yourself these days?'

Further reading

The World Economy in Transition by Michael Beenstock
(Allen & Unwin, 1983) is a daring broad sweep over the
problems discussed in this and the next two chapters. On de-
industrialization, see *Britain's Economic Problem: Too Few
Producers* by R. Bacon and W. A. Eltis (Macmillan, 2nd edn,
1980) – the book which popularized the whole debate about
the future of manufacturing employment. As an antidote, see
De-industrialisation, edited by Frank Blackaby (Heinemann,
1979).

4 Protectionism – who does it hurt?

One of the most disturbing features of the recession of the late 1970s and early 1980s has been the revival of protectionism. It is alarming because it is generally agreed that the collapse of world trade helped to spread the great depression in the 1930s from country to country. The growth of world trade since the Second World War, strongly encouraged by the dismantling of international trade barriers, has been closely linked with the growth of individual economies in the industrial world. [1–4]*

In the years after the First World War, in a climate of political and economic nationalism, governments reacted to the contraction of their domestic economies by throwing up tariff walls. Tariffs rose through the 1920s. The famous Smoot-Hawley Act which took effect in the USA in 1930 led to another round of tariff increases in other countries. These beggar-thy-neighbour policies undoubtedly helped to exacerbate the collapse of world trade which took place between 1929 and 1932.

Now the trade barriers are going up again. But this time they are being erected in a different way. During the depression, governments openly turned to tariffs – and quotas – as a cure for their economic problems. This time, protectionism is a much more surreptitious affair. Governments have publicly abjured it. Instead they enter into all kinds of secret and 'voluntary' arrangements with the country whose goods they want to keep out, and they target the measures on a small group of products or a single country. Protectionism this time is not open and across-the-board; rather it is discriminatory, covert and *ad hoc*.

Protectionism is the central theme of this chapter. The

* Before reading this chapter you may find it useful to refresh your understanding of the textbook importance of free trade. Questions 1–4 will assist in this.

interesting question is, why has protectionism revived so strongly? Why have governments turned to a solution which they know very well is profoundly dangerous to the health of the world economy, and not necessarily beneficial to their own country's economy? To this, there are two broad answers. One is that the longest recession since the war has driven Western governments to look for ways of sheltering their economies while they try to revive them. The other is that there has been a subtle shift in the balance of economic power between the developing countries and the Western world.

The first explanation of protectionism is undoubtedly the more important. Faced with a collapse of world trade, brought about by the cumulative impact of the deflationary policies of most industrial countries, individual governments have tried to protect key industries. But this is a relatively new phenomenon. It explains the sharp increase in trade issues – and the new friction in relations among the developed countries – which has marked the early 1980s. Even before the recession, though, there were signs that protectionism was gathering pace, and that countries were looking for ways of protecting their industries which would escape the formal rules drawn up after the Second World War. This earlier 'creeping protectionism' was aimed very largely at those Third World countries which had enjoyed a surge of growth in the 1970s.

This growth was one of the most interesting and important new economic developments of the 1970s. What happened was that a group of developing countries broke away from the pack, and achieved faster rates of growth, and sometimes faster growth of income per head, than the industrial countries. [5] Some of them are oil exporters. But the most remarkable ones have been tagged the Newly Industrialized Countries (NICs), and most of them are in Latin America or Southeast Asia.

Nobody is quite sure what caused this growth. It coincided with the big move from country to towns. It may have had something to do with the educational revolution. Levels of literacy in Hong Kong and South Korea are now close to those in the industrialized world. Even where there is still a noticeable gap some countries (Brazil, Mexico, Singapore) are almost at the point passed in the industrial countries only twenty years ago.

79

Agricultural growth may have contributed. It turned out to be faster than most people had expected partly, perhaps, because more aid was concentrated on helping the rural poor and less on prestige projects like dams and railways. Rapid agricultural growth goes hand in hand, in a developing country, with growth in the economy as a whole: the land is the main source of savings, of new consumers, of tax revenue.

Whatever the cause, the result has been a revolution (see Table 5). In a number of developing countries, manufacturing now accounts for a larger share of Gross Domestic Product than agriculture. They include Hong Kong (of course), Singapore (where agriculture constitutes only 1 per cent of GDP — or half the proportion in the United Kingdom) and Mexico. But a surprisingly large number of other countries, especially in South America, are rapidly approaching this point.

The result has dramatically affected the pattern of Third World trade. In 1958 manufactures were only about 5 per cent of the exports of non-industrial to industrial countries. By 1980 manufactures made up almost as large a proportion of the exports of the oil-importing Third World as primary

Table 5 Manufacturing as a proportion of Gross Domestic Product in a sample of developing and developed economies (%)

	1960	1980
India	14	18
Egypt	20	28*
South Korea	14	28
Mexico	19	24
Hong Kong	26	27*
Singapore	12	28
Greece	16	19
Yugoslavia	36	30*
Japan	34	29*
Germany	40	37
United States	29	24
United Kingdom	32	22

* 1979 figures

Source: *World Development Report 1982*, published for the World Bank by Oxford University Press, 1982, p. 114–15

products (excluding fuels). The great bulk of Third World manufactured exports is still accounted for by a tiny group of countries: in 1978 three countries, with less than 3 per cent of the developing world's population, supplied more than 40 per cent of its total manufactured exports. But the really interesting thing about the industrial revolution now under way in the Third World is the sheer numbers of countries whose economic structures are already being transformed beyond recognition.

Now from the point of view of the developing industrialists, this is good news. World markets for agriculture and other primary products are notoriously volatile. It is hard for anyone in an industrial country to imagine what it must feel like to depend for the bulk of one's export earnings on a commodity whose price may halve one year and double two years later. [6] The market for manufactured goods is wider, more likely to expand, and much more stable in terms of price. But for the developed countries, the revolution has brought with it serious problems of adjustment. There is an arresting quotation at the beginning of a recent report on the impact of protectionism in the developing countries from the West Indian economist, Arthur Lewis: 'The first business of all trading nations must be to try to keep industrial trade continually expanding, for unless it is expanding, the changes in the relative importance of countries which circumstances continually demand cannot be achieved without friction.' In the 1970s we saw substantial changes in the relative importance of some countries in some industries – and a gradual but dangerous winding down of the pace of expansion of international trade.

The consequent friction has built up mainly over trade in manufactured goods. Looked at from a broad angle, Third World manufactured imports into the developed countries are still chicken feed. But in some countries with long links with the Third World, levels of penetration have become much higher: in the UK the developing countries account for about 5 per cent of consumption of manufactured goods and in the Netherlands over 7 per cent, compared with, say, $1\frac{1}{2}$ per cent in Japan. Moreover in the early 1970s their penetration was growing very fast – at about 13 per cent a year in 1970–4 (see Table 6).

In some specific sectors – textiles, footwear, steel, electrical and electronic goods – penetration has been greater. The developing countries are inevitably most competitive in those labour-intensive industries where low wage costs are important. But in the developed countries, these industries are often precisely the ones located in declining regions where unemployment is already high. Sometimes even the new industries moving into these areas (think of electronics) are the very ones to which Third World industrialists are most likely to graduate.

It has been suggested by Michael Beenstock in *The World Economy in Transition* that de-industrialization in the West and the rise the NICs are related. The rise of manufacturing in the Third World has created profitable new investment opportunities which have attracted capital from the slow-growing West. Hence the rise of borrowing by the Third World (see chapter 5). The increase in the world supply of manufactures

Table 6 Imports of manufactures from developing countries by industrial countries, 1962–80

Industrial countries	1962	1970	1975	1980
	Imports of manufactures as % of GNP			
All industrial countries	4.1	6.2	7.7	9.6
Europe	7.7	11.1	12.6	15.2
Germany	5.9	8.8	9.7	12.4
Japan	2.3	2.3	2.1	2.6
United States	1.2	2.6	2.3	4.9
	% of imports of manufactures from developing countries			
All industrial countries	5.3	6.8	10.0	13.1
Europe	4.2	4.8	7.5	9.6
Germany	4.6	6.3	10.8	12.9
Japan	5.9	11.4	21.4	25.1
United States	12.3	14.7	21.0	26.7

Source: *World Development Report 1982*

lowered their price relative to raw materials, and depressed manufacturing in the developed countries compared with the service sector.

This thesis, which I have sketched very briefly (I have already referred to it in chapter 3 on page 59), presents a number of problems. In particular, has the rise in Third World manufactured trade really been large enough to have had such a big impact on manufacturing jobs in the developed countries? And if the NICs have had such an impact, why did the rise of Japan in the 1960s not have the same effect? Japan's exports of manufactures in 1981 were more than one and a half times as much as those of the seven leading NICs put together (Brazil, Hong Kong, Korea, Mexico, Singapore, Taiwan and Yugoslavia).

But the thesis does underline the impact that the spurt in Third World industrialization has had in some sectors. The point which is worth underlining is that the competition has been most fierce in the industries which are labour intensive, and which in the West employ the young, the unskilled and the disadvantaged. Moreover, these industries tend to be precisely the ones − in the West − which are least flexible and least innovative. That makes them yet more vulnerable to the new competition from the Third World.

The result has been a build-up of protectionist pressure. Yet at the same time, the formal structure of world trade has continued to become more liberal. As the industrial powers have taken down their visible fences, they have been erecting less visible but equally powerful new obstacles to trade. [7]

The formal structure is based on a code of rules administered by GATT − the General Agreement on Tariffs and Trade − which was set up after the Second World War to prevent a recurrence of the global protectionism of the 1930s. GATT's key principle is that any concession made by one trading country should be extended to all its trading partners on exactly the same basis as it is offered to the most favoured partner. This principle − known as 'm.f.n.' (most favoured nation) − has ensured that concessions wrested by the strong from the strong are also passed on to the weak. It has been crucial to the multi-lateral liberalism which is GATT's ideal.

Within GATT there has been a succession of rounds of

multilateral horse-trading under which tariffs have been cut on the m.f.n. principle to a point where, at the end of the 1970s, world trade was probably as unfettered as it had been at any time in history. The last batch of cuts − the Tokyo Round − take effect in stages up to the beginning of 1987. But even before the Tokyo agreement, GATT's ideal of generalized generosity had been eroded.

There had been three main departures from the principle. First, there had been a persistent failure to liberalize agricultural trade. Most developed countries, all through the postwar period, protected their farmers, often by underwriting the price paid for farm products or by subsidizing exports or both. This had some astonishing effects: the biggest exporter of rice to the Common Market, by a long chalk, is the United States. And American ground nut producers receive prices more than double those in Senegal, a major African producer, while the EEC price of soyabeans is about four times that of Brazil. [8]

The second hole in the GATT principle of non-discrimination was the establishment of the Common Market, a trading bloc in which the industrial countries offered each other special privileges. Subsequently, the Third World countries have negotiated two major trading agreements with the developed countries (the Generalized System of Preferences and the Lome Convention) which allow some exports into developed countries on preferential terms, without requiring the developing countries to reciprocate.

Finally in 1962 came the long-term Agreement on Cotton Textiles, the first important instance when GATT rules were formally set aside for entirely pragmatic reasons to hold down the growth of imports from developing producers into the industrial countries. The cotton textiles arrangement was broadened, in 1973, into the Multifibre Arrangements (MFA) which covered both wool and man-made fibre textiles and clothing as well as cotton. The fact that these arrangements have been negotiated under the shelter of GATT − though in flagrant breach of its rules − has done more to weaken GATT's standing in the eyes of Third World countries than anything else.

In the course of the 1970s, there was an accelerating growth of non-tariff barriers: constraints to trade barely envisaged when GATT was founded, and poorly covered by its rules. The main growth has been in what trade buffs call 'OMAs' and 'VERs' — orderly marketing arrangements and voluntary export restraints. Both are polite names for inter-governmental arm-twisting. They usually refer to quotas, negotiated informally, not approved or even discussed by parliament, sometimes kept secret from the rest of the world, and accepted under threat of even more severe measures of protection. The other big growth area has been in domestic government policies with an impact on trade: regional subsidies, for instance (preferred by developed countries to the more blatantly anti-social technique of export subsidies); export credit guarantees; technical standards which are peculiarly appropriate to a country's domestic suppliers; and government purchasing regulations which insist on products with a big input of domestic labour.

Monitoring measures of this kind — let alone measuring their effect — is almost impossible. One study which took a stab at it concluded that the proportion of OECD imports of manufactures affected by non-tariff restraints may have risen from about 4 per cent in 1974 to 17 per cent in 1980 (S. A. B. Page, 'The revival of protectionism and its consequences for Europe', *Journal of Common Market Studies*, September 1981). But GATT, the organization best placed to measure the growth of protectionism, has never tried: for the good reasons that a lot of non-tariff barriers are deliberately kept secret, and that it is not always easy to decide which domestic policy measures can rightly be counted as protectionism.

It does seem, however, as if the pace of protectionism may have been stepped up at the beginning of the 1980s. It may be that the developed countries are increasingly keeping out not just the products of Third World exporters but those of other industrial countries as well. For instance, the USA has severely limited its domestic market for all imports of foreign steel, while the collapse of world food prices has made the issue of agricultural protection the cause of an acrimonious dispute between the United States and the Common Market. Japan, inevitably, has been on the receiving end of a whole range of programmes of 'voluntary' restraint, especially on its exports of cars.

Still, it is Third World exports to the industrial countries which bear the brunt of non-tariff barriers. This is partly because non-tariff barriers impinge particularly on trade in clothing and textiles, and the textile trade is especially important to the Third World. One estimate (from the Page study, quoted above) is that about 30 per cent of OECD manufactured imports from developing countries were affected by non-tariff barriers in 1979, compared with about 11 per cent of trade in manufactures within the OECD itself.

It is a reasonable bet that non-tariff barriers might have become more important even without the aggravating effect of the recession. For as trade in goods becomes more sophisticated, the importance of price diminishes. People buy a washing machine today not necessarily because it is the cheapest on the market, but because it has the best reputation for reliability, or because it is in stock and they do not have to wait for it to be delivered. This would probably have reduced the effectiveness of tariffs even if international negotiations had not concentrated so heavily on removing that particular restraint to trade.

At the same time, the tendency of governments has been to intervene more and more in the management of the economy — to 'pick winners', to cushion the decline of older industries and regions, to protect the environment and to fix health and safety standards. But there is sometimes a thin line between measures taken to help old industries to adjust or to set sensible standards for domestic producers . . . and measures whose implicit aim is to hold foreign competitors at bay.

Protectionism is fundamentally a way of trying to slow down the pace of adjustment. The pressures for adjustment in the 1970s were by no means predominantly caused by the rise of Third World industrialists. The huge rise in relative energy prices was at least as important. And the worldwide recession aggravated the pressures on some industries. It also made it possible for them to defend themselves by arguing that their problems were cyclical, rather than structural, and would pass when the recession passed. Steel is a good example. The industry was hit in the 1970s and early 1980s from several directions at once: by higher energy prices, by the rapid build-up of new (and therefore more efficient) capacity in developing countries, and by the collapse of demand. It was not easy to see clearly how far the right policy was to preserve steel-making capacity in the hope that world demand would revive – and how far to close it down, on the assumption that new demand would be met more cheaply by other countries.

It is this diffusion of pressures which makes protectionism seem an attractive short-term solution in the thick of a recession. But short-term solutions have a way of becoming long-term. And the benefits of protectionism are much more concentrated and obvious than the costs. Politicians rarely defend protectionism as a global solution. They tend to say, 'Of course we need to defend free trade, but when I see what is happening to the steel industry. . . .' The benefits of pro-tectionism accrue to individual industries – or even to individual firms. The costs are widely distributed among consumers, in ways which may be very hard to identify.

That may be the reason why so many measures of protection apply to consumer goods – to cars, to televisions, to video recorders, to clothes and shoes – rather than to producer goods like machine tools and semi-manufactured goods, for instance. Consumers are an inefficient lobby – unlike pro-ducers. But protectionism invariably and inevitably raises the prices consumers have to pay. That is the way it works. And because protectionism is usually aimed at keeping out goods which are undercutting domestic producers, it usually hurts the poor most. The Consumers' Association has demonstrated this point with an estimate that the Multifibre Arrangements put up the price of basic imported clothes by between 15 and 40 per cent ('The price of protection', Consumers' Associ-ation, 1979). That is a lot more than Sir Geoffrey Howe's notorious increase in Value Added Tax – although it attracted much less political outrage.

Moreover, that increase in prices to consumers may not necessarily buy protection for the domestic industry. It may simply result in the substitution of high-cost imports for low cost imports. That is what happened to the British car industry, where imports from Japan, restrained by 'voluntary' agree-ment, were largely replaced with imports from the Common Market; and it has happened with imports of clothing from the developing countries too. Even if domestic producers are bought some respite in their home market, the cost may be a fiercer battle in export markets, whose consumers will reap the benefit of more strenuous price competition. But consumers are typically badly organized, while producers under pressure are expert at lobbying governments. A politician finds it easier to think of the people who lose their jobs as a direct result of foreign competition than of the thousands of pounds it may cost to preserve each job in terms of spending power foregone. [9]

But there is a further argument against protectionism which is rather more complex. Controls on imports allow domestic producers to charge higher prices for their goods than they would be able to do if faced with unrestricted foreign competition. That is the counterpart of the damage done to consumer incomes by import controls. It also means that the profits of firms producing goods which compete with imports are protected. But firms producing exports enjoy no such protection. They cannot raise their prices on world markets – especially in a major world recession. They may find the prices of their inputs raised by the protected producers. For instance, when the USA and the Common Market reached an agreement to protect domestic steel producers in 1978, there were increases in the price of steel which greatly exacerbated the problems of producers of cars, for which steel represents about 18 per cent of the value of the finished product.

The squeeze on exporters' profit margins is likely to mean a contraction in their industries, to the benefit of firms whose products compete with imports. It is impossible, in other words, to protect a whole economy from foreign competition. It may be possible to protect individual industries – but only at a cost: in terms of consumer welfare, and of the success of exporting industries. Protection cannot increase overall employment; it can only redistribute it at a lower level of national wealth.

If it is true that there is a fundamental structural adjustment taking place between the economies of the Third World and of the developing countries, then protectionism might appear an attractive way of slowing down the process. But the danger is that it will make the adjustment process more painful by distorting the development of both the rich countries and the poor. We have just seen the way in which protectionism may save import-competing industries in a developed economy at the expense of exporting industries. But the developing economy, on the receiving end of protection, may also be distorted. If protection holds down the export profits to be made in, say, the clothing industry, that may divert capital into sectors with a 'second-best' return: leather goods, perhaps, or simple engineering.

There is some evidence that this is exactly what has been happening. The MFA has proved a very effective way of holding down exports of textiles, in which Third World countries have a clear comparative advantage, into other sectors where trade restrictions are fewer. In the ten years up to 1973, developing countries' exports of clothing to the developed countries grew by 21 per cent a year. Then came the MFA. In 1973–6 clothing exports rose by only $14\frac{1}{2}$ per cent a year. And by 1977–8 the industrial countries' imports of engineering products from the developing countries were growing almost twice as fast as their imports of textiles and clothing.

Because protectionism is most likely to be applied against those industries in which developing producers have the greatest comparative advantage over producers in developed countries, it is likely to hold back precisely those industries which are the best bet for Third World investment. Money and manpower will be diverted into second-best projects: into producing substitutes for imports, perhaps, instead of goods to sell abroad. And when that happens, the demand for imports often tends to outrun a country's export earnings, forcing it to rein in expansion – and making even second-best projects less profitable than might reasonably have been expected.

At the margin, protectionism will make the repayment of Third World debt, the subject of the next chapter, a bit more difficult. At the margin, it will force the developing countries to cut back their imports from the developed world. The gravest danger is that protectionism will become more than marginal. Begun in response to the recession, it will suddenly gather momentum and have a real and substantial effect on the length and depth of the depression. [10]

For one of the main consequences of the tremendous post-war progress towards freer trade has been that the world's economies are more dependent on each other than ever before. Precisely because foreign trade has grown faster than GNP in the OECD countries throughout the post-war era, both exports and imports account for a larger share of GNP than ever before. The result has been that the domestic economies of the industrial economies are more vulnerable than they have ever been to what happens elsewhere.

The industrial countries still run a hefty trade surplus in manufactured goods with the Third World. Even excluding the growth of exports to OPEC, the surplus has been increasing since 1973 by more than 5 per cent a year in real terms. Developing countries now buy roughly a quarter of the merchandise exports of the industrial world — 45 per cent of those of the United States, 38 per cent of those of Japan, 25 per cent of those of the UK. Thus are the interests of the First World and the Third harnessed together. [11]

Questions

[1] Comparative advantage

The theory of comparative advantage is still the centre-piece of textbook chapters on international trade. The theory was developed by David Ricardo (1772–1823) and is still taught today. It is also still used for one of its original purposes: to demonstrate that trade is to the advantage of poor no less than rich nations.

'Under a system of perfectly free commerce, each country naturally devoted its capital and labour to such employments as are most beneficial to each — it is the principle which determines that wine shall be made in France and Portugal, that corn shall be grown in America and Poland, and that hardware and other goods shall be manufactured in England.'
The Works and Correspondence of David Ricardo,
P. Sraffa (ed.) Cambridge University Press, 1962, p. 133

Ricardo then set about demonstrating that even if one country could not produce anything more cheaply (in terms of labour time) than another, it would still be to the benefit of both countries to specialize and then do a swap. He took Portugal and England as examples, and with what, at his time, was an amazingly tactful gesture to the Portuguese produced this first model of comparative advantage:

	Product of one unit of labour in cloth weaving	Product of one unit of labour in wine making
England	10	8
Portugal	11	12

i   *What pattern of specialization and exchange does this model suggest would be possible?*

[2]   The benefits of free trade

Economists have clung to the notion of allowing comparative advantage to operate freely because they believe there to be a net benefit to the world community in doing so.

	One unit of resources can produce	
	Wheat (bushels)	Cloth (metres)
America	200	120
India	10	20

This model shows that America has the absolute advantage in the production of both wheat and cloth. Can it, therefore, have anything to gain from trading with relatively inefficient India?

i   *In the production of which product does America have the greatest comparative advantage?*

ii   *Assume now that America decides to move one-tenth of a unit of resources into wheat production from cloth production. By how much will the production of wheat and cloth alter in America?*

iii *Equally, assume India transfers one unit of resources
from wheat into cloth production — with what effect on the
production of wheat and cloth in India?*

iv *Now complete this table:*

	Change in production due to specialization	
	Wheat (bushels)	Cloth (metres)
America		
India		
World		

This model is seen to increase world output of wheat and
cloth. Specialization makes more goods available in the world
and, providing the two countries can establish mutually
beneficial 'swap rates', the standard of living of both must
rise.

v *For the specialization to occur, however, India has to
transfer 10 times as many resources from one industry to the
other as America does. What structural problems might this
present in India?*

[3] Terms of trade

In the previous question India concentrated her productive
resources into cloth manufacture. Moving one unit of resources
from wheat production means that India sacrifices 10 units of
wheat but gains 20 units of cloth. When it comes to trade,
India will benefit as long as every 20 units of cloth traded gain
her more than 10 units of wheat.

America on the other hand will trade her surplus wheat for
cloth. To gain 20 metres of cloth America has to transfer one-
sixth of a unit of resources and these could have made 33 units
of wheat. So as long as America is never asked to give up more
than 33 units of wheat to gain 20 units of cloth, she will find
the terms of trade benefit her.

i   This can be summarized to provide the acceptable terms of trade in this example:
    a   America will give up to ? units of wheat to get hold of 20 units of cloth.
    b   India wants more than ? units of wheat to give up 20 units of cloth.

ii If the prevailing terms of trade in this case are such that 15 units of wheat are traded for 20 units of cloth, who derives the greatest benefit from international trade?

[4] Changes in the terms of trade

Normally the terms of trade are not expressed in the sense of the exchange of physical amounts of products. They are usually shown as:

index of export prices
─────────────────────
index of import prices

Country A is a developing African nation; it has a rapidly growing population and a desperate need to import food but it is favoured with oil deposits. It sells 100 units of oil for 50 world currency units each. Its total trade revenue is, therefore, 5000 wcu. With this it buys food at 10 wcu per unit.

i   How many food units does Country A buy?

ii What are the physical terms of trade in this case?

A poor grain harvest in North America results in an increase in the world price of food — it goes up to 12 wcu per unit.

iii How much food can country A buy with its oil revenue?

iv What options are open to Country A in this situation where the terms of trade have moved against it?

v   If the country decides to increase its oil production why might this lead to a further deterioration in its terms of trade?

[5] GDP and the standard of living

An island economy has a population of 10,000,000 and its Gross Domestic Product is $4000 million.

i   What is its per capita GDP? How does this compare to that of the UK?

In the course of one year GDP rises to $4144 million and the population growth rate is 5% pa.

ii   What is its per capita GDP now?

iii   Why, despite an economic growth rate of 4% pa, has the standard of living dropped?

iv   If per capita GDP was $400, does this mean that every citizen of the island has an income of $400? What else do you really need to know to make judgements about the average standard of living?

The government decides that it will appropriate the increase in GDP — so it raises taxes to pull in the $144 million. It spends this on the provision of increased hospital services at a cost of $4000 per hospital bed. This provides 36,000 beds or 1 bed per 278 members of the population.

v   What would you now say had happened to the standard of living in this country, bearing in mind that average disposable income will now be lower?

vi   Asked to write an article comparing the standard of living in the following countries:
New Zealand
Zimbabwe
Hungary
what factors would you concentrate on when making your comparisons?

[6]   Agricultural product markets

The supply of wheat is always determined by the previous season's prices — in the sowing season, when farmers plan their next year's crops, the only information they have is the price they got paid for products this year (see table opposite).

i   When this market clears what will be
– the price?
* the level of supply?*
* the level of demand?*
* farmers' total income?*

World price of wheat ($)	World supply of wheat (following year)	World demand for wheat
10	100	145
11	110	140
12	120	135
13	130	130
14	140	125
15	150	120
16	160	115
17	170	110

A bad harvest now reduces the supply of wheat to 125 units.

ii   At what price does the market now clear and what level of income results for farmers?

Higher prices and incomes cause supplies to increase in the following year — farmers observe the high prices for wheat in this season and decide to move out of the production of other products and into the growing of wheat.

iii   Given that the market clearing price was $14 this year, what will the level of supply be for next year?

iv   What will now happen to farmers' income?

v   Can you deduce the price, output and income cycles which will occur in this market from now on?

vi   You might expect wheat farmers to adjust their behaviour since they constantly seem to be losing out. What part of economic analysis supports the view that one wheat farmer is unlikely to do this?

vii   Why is the demand for agricultural products:
a   relatively unresponsive to price changes?
b   unlikely to rise in direct proportion to increases in GDP?

[7]   Forms of protection

There are basically two types of protection measures:
a   tariffs — which are effectively taxes on imports

Figure 16 UK market for imports

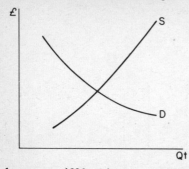

b non-tariff barriers — any intervention in trade which is not a tariff; for example, insisting on certain technical standards

They both have the same effect: they increase the supply price of imports.

i Reconstruct the market model (Figure 16), showing the effect of the imposition of a protective measure.

ii If the protective measure was introduced to improve the balance of payments by reducing the value of imports, upon what does the success of the policy depend?

iii Under what circumstances will the imposition of a protective measure fail to improve the balance of payments?

[8] Export restitution payments — Common Agricultural Policy

'Export Refund — may be granted by the Commission when the world prices are significantly lower than EEC prices to maintain the competitive position of EEC exporters on the world market.'

Farm Finance in the EEC, Barclays Bank

i Given that European farmers are known to be high-cost producers of many agricultural products, what do you understand by the phrase 'maintain the competitive position'?

Consider the levy and refund system for wheat in the EEC (Figure 17). In a year when the wheat harvest is good the world

Figure 17 Levy and refund system for wheat

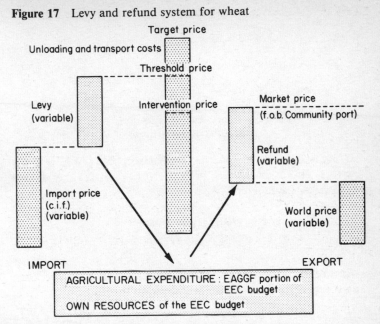

Source: 'The agricultural policy of the European Community', *European Documentation Periodical*, February 1979, p. 13

price of wheat will be low and world suppliers will be seeking markets for their surplus.

ii *Explain how the variable import levy operates − does it stop imports of wheat?*

iii *What does the EEC do with the money derived from the import levy?*

iv *Without the levy and refund protection system, what would have happened to European farmers − with what effect on next year's supply and price of wheat?*

v *Assume that one unit of account (u.a.) = £0.0885. Look at Table 7 (p. 98) and estimate how much sterling was spent by the Community on agriculture protection.*

The population of Malawi is 6 million. GNP per head is $140. Malawi's principal exports are agricultural products − sugar,

Table 7 Community expenditure in support of agriculture 1977*

Guarantee section (6662 million u.a.)	%
Storage and withdrawal from the market	18
Export refunds	41
Price subsidies and guidance premiums	41

* From the European agricultural guarantee and guidance fund

Source: Farm Finance in the EEC, Barclays Bank

tea, ground nuts. Observe the comparison between how much the EEC pays to protect its farmers from countries like Malawi and the total income of Malawi.

[9] Who benefits from trade barriers?

A country imports 50,000 family saloon cars every year at a price of £5000 each. Price elasticity of demand for imported cars is estimated at 1.2 − a 10% increase in prices would have the effect of reducing demand by 12%.

A domestic car plant employs 5000 workers with average annual earnings being £7000. The plant produces family saloon cars at a price of £6000 each and is threatened with closure because it cannot compete with cheap imports.

Pressure is successfully brought to bear upon the government which introduces a tariff on imported cars, the effect of which is to raise the price of these cars to £6000. The car plant is duly saved.

The question now becomes − is the country 'better off' as a result of the introduction of the tariff? Do you think the income benefit of protecting jobs at the car plant is greater or less than the real income loss when the average price of cars went up?

There is enough information here for you to produce an argument. Does the country benefit from the introduction of the tariff? What other factors might have to be considered?

[10] Terms of trade − unequal exchange

In his speech to the non-aligned countries' summit in 1983, President Fidel Castro of Cuba made the following points:

'With the decline in commodity prices and the continuing high prices for manufactures and oil, the inevitable result is the worsening of unequal exchange affecting most of the Third World. To illustrate this phenomenon here are some examples:

In 1960, 6.3 tons of oil could be purchased with the sale of a ton of sugar. In 1982 only 0.7 tons of oil could be bought with the same amount of sugar.

In 1960, 37.3 tons of fertilizers could be bought for a ton of coffee. In 1982 only 15.8 tons could be bought.

In 1959, the sale of 6 tons of jute fibre could buy a 7–8 ton truck. By late 1982, 26 tons of jute fibre were needed to buy the same truck.

In 1959, one ton of copper wire could buy 39 X-ray tubes for medical purposes. By late 1982, only three X-ray tubes could be bought with that same ton.

These terms of trade are repeated on most of our export commodities, and this situation is coupled with the growing protectionism in Western markets against exports from the Third World. Added to the traditional tariff barriers there is now a wide range of non-tariff barriers.'

The Guardian, 25 March 1983

Fidel Castro is here drawing attention to the way the terms of trade have moved against Third World countries in the past two decades.

i   *What is the formal method of calculating the terms of trade?*

ii   *Can you offer reasons as to why the prices of the internationally traded goods have changed in the way indicated above?*

iii   *If a country had a requirement for 5000 medical X-ray tubes annually and obtained them by exporting copper wire, what increase in exports would have to occur if the country was to maintain its X-ray provision?*

[11] The shifting balance of the world economy

Figure 18 shows how the world's rate of growth of economic activity slowed substantially in the 1970s. The performance of

Figure 18   The shifting balance of the world economy

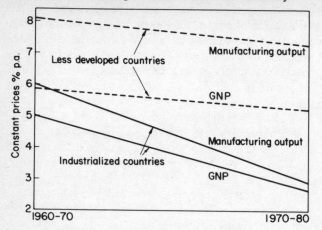

Source: *The Guardian*, 20 October 1982

manufacturing output in the less developed countries is substantially different from what happened in the major industrialized countries.

i   *What difference will there be between less developed countries and industrialized countries in terms of the relative importance of manufacturing output at the end of the period compared to the beginning?*

ii   *What has been the response of the industrialized countries to this shifting balance? Do you think they have reacted reasonably?*

Further reading

The most interesting regular survey of world trade problems appears in the annual GATT report (*GATT International Trade 1981/82* is the most recent, published November 1982 and available from GATT Secretariat, Centre William Rappard,

154 rue de Lausanne, 1211 Geneva 21, Switzerland — free for students). For the Third World in particular, see also the annual *World Development Report*, published each August by the World Bank (1818 H Street NW, Washington, DC 20433, USA) and also available from Oxford University Press. The 1983 edition costs £5.95 paperback.

5 Third World debt – is it repayable?

In August 1982 some of the world's most marble-halled, blue-chip banks wondered for a few days whether they might go bust. The cause of their nightmares was Mexico. In the space of a few days, it emerged that Mexico had run up foreign debts of some $83 billion, most of them to commercial banks – and that it simply did not have the foreign exchange earnings to continue to pay the interest on those debts, and to repay those which were falling due and not being renewed.

Several US banks, it transpired, had made loans to Mexico larger than their entire capital. The Bank of Tokyo, one of Japan's largest, had lent the equivalent of 80 per cent of its capital to this single Latin American state. Mexico owed the banks more than any other developing country. But it was at once clear that there was a small number of countries, most of them in Latin America, on the verge of a similar cash crisis. One of them, Brazil, had outstanding loans almost as large as Mexico's.

It is with the origins of this crisis and with its possible aftermath that this chapter is concerned. How on earth did the banks, which never seem anxious to lend money to anyone as credit-worthy as you and I, manage to get themselves into such a situation? What are its longer-term implications? One important point to bear in mind is that what happens to the financial system is partly the result of what happens in what Denis Healey used to call the 'real' economy. But at the same time, shocks to the financial system can reinforce shocks to the real economy. There is a sort of reverberation between the two.

The roots of the 1982 crisis are in a massive change which took place ten years earlier in the way countries – especially developing countries – raised money. In the course of the 1960s, the larger commercial banks hit on a way of lending dollars to foreign companies and countries without being constrained by American exchange controls. The money they lent was Eurodollars. It consisted of dollars held outside the United States. For instance, when a US company paid a foreign supplier, the supplier might deposit those dollars at a bank branch outside the US, and that transformed them into Eurodollars. The bank might well be operating from an office in London and might be American, British, or even the Moscow Narodny. It could lend the Eurodollars to somebody else. As long as they were not deposited in a domestic US account, or used to invest in the US, they remained Eurodollars.

At this stage most Eurodollar loans were to individual companies, or to finance trade or particular investment projects. Occasionally a big industrial country raised a Eurodollar loan to cover its balance of payments deficit. But it was only with the first big rise of the oil price in 1973–4 that lending to the Eastern bloc countries, and the Third World, really took off. From taking a tiny share of Euromarket loans, these two groups became large borrowers, in some years accounting for half or just over half of all syndicated loans.

The effect was an absolute transformation in the type of loans the average big commercial bank would have on its books. In the course of the 1970s, the proportion of foreign assets and liabilities of the banks, relative to their total assets and liabilities, rose in the OECD countries as a group from 12 per cent to about 22 per cent. In other words, the importance of foreign borrowers to the total business of the banks of the industrial world nearly doubled in a decade. Bankers who, in the late 1960s, would have thought it quite exotic to make a loan for a factory in Frankfurt or an office in Ohio suddenly found themselves lending millions of dollars to places they could hardly find on the map, let alone pronounce.

For it was the growth in loans to Third World borrowers which was most extraordinary (see Figure 19). It is hard to realize now that as recently as 1971 two-thirds of the external debt of developing countries was owed to official sources – mainly to governments and to international aid agencies. Some of the remaining third was borrowed not from banks but from companies which had sold goods to the Third World. A developing country, contemplating the building of a new

Figure 19 Growth of bank lending to non-OPEC LDCs (% change in banks' claim in dollar terms)

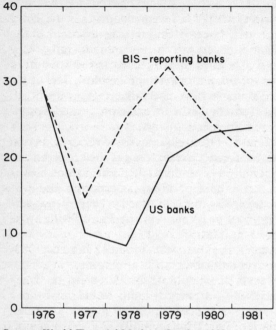

Source: *World Financial Markets*, October 1982

power station or port, applied not to the Eurodollar market but to the World Bank, whose job was essentially to supply money to finance development. If the country ran up a current account deficit, it might turn to the International Monetary Fund – but the main job of the IMF was lending money to the industrial countries to bail them out of their (much larger) balance of payments problems.

By the early 1980s all that had changed. So important had bank lending to the Third World become that by 1982 the leading US banks had outstanding loans to the developing world twice as large as their total capital. Depending a bit on how you reckon it, the entire outstanding sum of Third World debt was somewhere over $500 billion. The reason why this mountain grew up is that two things happened comfortably to coincide: the oil-induced deficits and the build-up of industrial growth in the Third World, on the one hand, and on the other the surplus funds of the oil exporters. The banks brought the two together. [1]

At the beginning of the 1970s, several countries in the Third World were in the early stages of an investment boom. In the subsequent decade (see chapter 4 for more details) they clocked up remarkable rates of growth: 6 per cent or more annually. But the growth paths were not identical. The newly industrialized countries (NICs) of Southeast Asia did it all rather differently from the NICs of Latin America. In Southeast Asia, the successful countries tended to restructure their economies much more towards exports (from 10 per cent to 60 per cent of Gross Domestic Product) than in the Latin American NICs (from 10 to 15 per cent of GDP). The difference was even more dramatic in terms of what was exported (the proportion of manufactured goods exported by Taiwan rose during the decade from 10 to 90 per cent, compared with a rise from 10 to 25 per cent in Mexico). [2]

Arguably (Gustav Ranis, *Financial Times*, 12 January 1983) Latin America set about its investment programme in a more vulnerable way than the Southeast Asian countries. They could – in some cases – afford to: they had a far richer stock of natural resources. But they also relied more on foreign capital imports, which paid for between 20 and 30 per cent of cumulative investment in Mexico, for example, compared with less than 10 per cent in Taiwan.

Countries have imported massive funds to pay for ambitious growth programmes before now. Testifying before a Senate committee in Washington, one US banker, Rimmer de Vries, pointed out that between 1870 and 1890 the USA ran current account deficits averaging almost 25 per cent of exports (*World Financial Markets*, February 1983, p. 2). During those two decades, it accumulated an external debt which averaged over 300 per cent of exports in the last five years of the period. Interest payments on the debts ranged between 10 and 15 per cent of exports. Those sort of figures would have put it straight into intensive care in 1982. But America in the nineteenth century was lucky: it did not have to contend with the sort of nominal interest rates which modern America has helped to inflict on the Third World.

The Third World needed to borrow; OPEC needed to invest. And the oil exporters liked the relative anonymity and flexibility of placing their surplus cash on deposit with the banks. When the 1973 oil price rises brought extra deposits streaming into the banks, it also left all oil-importing countries facing large current account deficits. Overnight, the banks became the main conduit through which the surplus oil revenues of OPEC were recycled.

It suited the banks very well. Lending to countries appeared to be a lot safer than lending to companies, which looked more risky than ever as the recession closed in. 'Companies fail, but countries do not', bankers told each other as they jetted from Argentina to Nigeria, from Poland to Yugoslavia. And indeed there had been very few occasions when a banker had had to write off a loan to a sovereign state, although some countries had occasionally been forced to reschedule (to postpone repayment). In the Eastern bloc, there was the added comfort of the thought that the Soviet Union would never allow one of its satellites to default.

The conjuring trick seemed to work. The twenty-one main developing country borrowers expanded their outstanding debt at an annual average of over 30 per cent between the mid-1970s and the end of 1979 (*World Financial Markets*, February 1983, p. 3). But their exports were also leaping ahead. In 1975 their total debt-to-exports ratio was 120 per cent. By the end of 1979, it had only risen to 130 per cent (respectable compared to the rakish progress of nineteenth-century America). [3]

It was with the December 1979 oil price rise − the second big oil shock − that things began to go wrong. Everyone who had predicted financial collapse after the 1973−4 oil price rise and been forced to retreat with egg on their faces now tended to assume that the banks would manage all right the second time around. So the banks went on lending, and their lending was more and more concentrated on a rather small group of Latin American countries which gave themselves a real national birthday treat. Bank lending to Mexico more than doubled between 1978 and 1982; lending to Argentina almost quadrupled.

But the aftermath of the second oil shock was different

from the first. The most important difference was the reaction of the industrial countries. In the mid-1970s, they had adopted a relatively relaxed fiscal and monetary stance. The result was that inflation remained high (which eroded the value of borrowing countries' debts) and interest rates remained low (which kept the cost of debt servicing under control).

The second time round, there was much more determination to stamp out inflation. What's more, in Britain and then in the USA, the task was given almost exclusively to monetary policy. Both countries initially made the appalling mistake of trying to squeeze monetary growth while allowing their fiscal deficits to increase. The effect of a monetary policy which made no attempt to accommodate the inflation caused directly by higher oil prices was inevitably a sharp decline in the rate of economic growth. The effect of trying to do everything with monetary policy alone was inevitably stratospheric interest rates.

So borrowers were caught in an awful pincer, between recession in their main export markets and soaring debt costs. For the first time in a quarter of a decade, world trade was stagnant for two years running – and declined in the third. Developing countries were hurt more badly than in any previous post-war recession. As demand began to contract, raw material prices collapsed, and for some commodities they fell to levels not seen since 1945. Oil prices went into headlong decline: good news for many developing countries and potentially stimulating for the West, but disastrous for some of the biggest borrowers who had been counting on their oil revenues as security against their debts. [**4, 5**]

Usually, one of the offsetting forces in a recession is a sharp fall in interest rates. But in this recession, interest rates initially went up. There are two key rates to which most international bank loans are pegged: three-month and six-month LIBOR. (The initials stand for London Inter-Bank Offered Rate, because the rate is the one at which banks are willing to offer spare funds on loan to other banks.) LIBOR (pronounced 'liebore') is the banks' jargon for the three- and six-month Eurodollar deposit rates; they had been just under $14\frac{1}{2}$ per cent in the immediate wake of the 1979 oil price rise. A year later, at the end of 1980, three-month LIBOR was $17\frac{1}{2}$ per cent: six-month, just under 16½ per cent. It was not until the closing days of 1982 that both came down to single figures. Even then, they remained very high relative to inflation.

The impact on borrowers with large debts was enormous. In the past, most developing country borrowing had been at fixed rates of interest. Now, a rapidly rising proportion of bank credits, especially to Argentina, Brazil, Korea and Mexico, the four really big borrowers, were at floating rates. So when interest rates rose, the debt service burden immediately increased.

Moreover, as interest rates rose higher, the maturity length of loans to the Third World shortened. To the banks, short-term loans looked a safer bet: if the going got rough, they thought they could always refuse to roll over the loan. So between the end of 1979 and the middle of 1982, short-term credits to developing countries grew by almost 30 per cent a year while bank lending in total was growing at an annual rate of rather over 20 per cent.

The effect of higher interest rates, more rapidly maturing debts and collapsing export earnings was bound to be disaster for someone. [6] For the twenty-one big Third World borrowers, the ratio of interest payments and maturing short-term debt to export earnings rocketed from 50 per cent in 1979 to 75 per cent during 1982 (see Table 8). Almost all net new borrowing in this period was by a handful of Latin American countries; and for five of them, owing between them almost half the developing world's debt to the banks of the main industrial countries, things were much worse. In 1982 their total debt service payments (interest payments plus maturing debt) came to more than their entire export earnings. For four others, the total came to 90 per cent or more of their export earnings (*World Financial Markets*, October 1982, p. 5).

Banks began to do nervous sums on the backs of envelopes. The OPEC surplus was evaporating more quickly this time around, as oil exporters stepped up their spending programmes. The inflow of deposits was slackening. Net new lending began to tail off. In 1980 came the Iranian hostage crisis, when the Americans froze Iranian foreign assets. That proved that it was not only nasty Third World regimes which could threaten the banks' cash. The following year, amid the

108

Table 8 Selected external financial indicators for 21 major LDC borrowers (group averages)

| | 21 LDCs | | | |
	Total	Latin America[1]	Asia[2]	Middle East[3] and Africa
Total external debt[4] as % of exports[5]				
1979	133	196	73	130
1980	123	182	70	113
1981	140	202	78	138
1982	172	259	94	155
Total debt service[6] as % of exports[5]				
1979	50	76	27	46
1980	47	73	27	38
1981	60	92	33	49
1982	75	125	38	56
Current account deficit as % of exports[5]				
1979	12	21	7	8
1980	12	22	8	5
1981	22	31	12	24
1982	23	33	14	23

[1] Argentina, Brazil, Chile, Colombia, Ecuador, Mexico, Peru, and Venezuela
[2] Indonesia, Korea, Malaysia, Philippines, Taiwan, and Thailand
[3] Algeria, Egypt, Ivory Coast, Morocco, Nigeria, and Turkey
[4] Average of beginning- and end-year debt levels
[5] Exports of goods and services
[6] Interest on total external debt plus all maturing debt, including amortization of medium- and long-term debt and all short-term debt

Source: *World Financial Markets*, February 1983, p. 6

turmoil of Solidarity's uprising, Poland threatened to default on more than \$13 billion of money owed to Western banks. That proved that even a dictatorship could not necessarily persuade people to accept peaceably a massive cut in their living standards in order to release enough net export earnings to pay off big debts.

Poland's near-default looked wistfully small the following

year. In August 1982, just as the world's bankers were packing their clean socks for their yearly jolly at the World Bank/ International Monetary Fund annual meeting, there came news that Mexico would not continue to make payments on its $83 billion of foreign debt. That was a bigger sum than the entire Comecon debt. Mexico had managed to run up the second-largest bank borrowings in the world, second only to Brazil, which was patently floundering too. In rapid succession, rescue packages had to be strung together for Argentina, Yugoslavia, Romania, Chile, Uruguay, Cuba, Venezuela. . . .

It must look a little odd, with hindsight, that the banks did not realize earlier the extent of the potential catastrophe. For if a large borrowing country had actually been allowed to declare a default – to announce that it was wiping the slate clean and beginning again – several large and respectable commercial banks would undoubtedly have been in dire trouble. No doubt they would have been rescued by their central bank: these days, central banks do not sit quietly by and allow big banks to go to the wall. But the whole international banking system has become so inter-linked that it would have been perfectly possible for a panic to have got out of hand. At the very least, a lot of smallish banks might have gone bust.

So how did banks become so embroiled? One reason is that in the mid-1970s, the business was immensely profitable. Another is the way the international financial markets had come to operate. At the end of the 1960s, the banks devised the technique of the syndicated loan. It works like this. One or more banks play the role of managers. They will stump up very little of the cash themselves, but will hawk the loan around other banks, asking them to take up a stake in the total. As the other banks may well be asking the 'lead' banks to chip in to one of their loans next week, they are usually happy to help. Even after the list is full, the participating banks may themselves pass on chunks of their share to other, smaller banks.

The number of banks involved in the syndicated loan market increased vastly in the course of the 1970s. One estimate by the World Bank reckoned that there were ten times as many institutions in it by 1982 as there had been a decade earlier – and that perhaps a third of the loan managers had headquarters outside Europe or North America, compared with only one eighth in 1973 (*Risks in International Bank Lending*, first report of the International Banking Study Group of the Group of Thirty, published by the Group of Thirty, New York, 1982). And as the number of banks grew, the whole business became more competitive. The margins banks earned on their loans were chiselled away. To keep up profits everyone tried to lend more. And everyone probably became a little less careful.

More important, no individual bank had the foggiest notion of how much an individual country was currently borrowing. There was no system for pooling information on who was lending how much to whom. The central banks had some idea, but not the people who were writing the cheques. As one economic commentator has put it, 'The fact that the international lending by the big banks has been financed by a gigantic chain letter has meant that "everyone's business is nobody's business".'

When it became apparent that Mexico might default, Arthur Burns, the former head of the US Federal Reserve, said wryly, 'The banks have been very foolish. We must now pray that they will go on being foolish.' For the only alternative to default was for Mexico to borrow more money. There was no way that the International Monetary Fund, the usual lifeboat for sinking countries, could afford a rescue: its entire available resources, at about $20 billion, looked puny beside Mexico's debts. Indeed, the Fund's main role has been to persuade the debtor to adopt wiser economic policies, and the banks to go on lending. Its own new loans have inevitably been small in comparison with the scale of Third World debt.

The idea of throwing bad money after bad appalled many bankers. But they were persuaded, or in some cases browbeaten, into submission by the International Monetary Fund and by their fellow bankers. The same technique has been used in subsequent country rescues. It is quite different from the way in which earlier reschedulings were handled. After Turkey rescheduled four times between 1978 and 1982, it found itself virtually shut out of the medium term loan market. After the 1981 Polish crisis, the entire Eastern bloc was virtually frozen out of the Euromarket.

It is still a highly risky policy, and a controversial one. The obvious risk is that the fragile structure of the financial market might suddenly be shaken by some crisis of confidence, bringing down a clutch of smaller and medium-sized banks and even perhaps a big one or two. That risk, as of spring 1983, appears to be increased by the way in which many loans to Third World countries have been financed.

For while the larger banks have paid for their lending mainly from the deposits of their customers, a great many smaller banks have relied heavily on borrowing in the interbank market – in using funds which other banks do not, for the moment, want and which they are willing to lend to another bank, usually for quite short periods of time. One study (J. G. Ellis, 'Eurobanks and the interbank market', Bank of England Quarterly Bulletin, September 1981) suggests that interbank deposits make up between two-thirds and three-quarters of all external and Eurocurrency deposits.

The danger is that if the market remains nervous, smaller banks will find it harder and harder to borrow the funds they need on the interbank market. And because of the way the market links good banks with bad in a vast, anonymous network, a problem in one part of the system might hurt perfectly sound banks. In the 1974 fringe banking crisis in Britain, even National Westminster had to issue a statement to deny rumours that the Bank of England had had to bail it out.

While bank failure may be the obvious risk, I am not very sure that it is the most likely one. In January 1983 Robin Leigh Pemberton, the Governor-designate of the Bank of England, said that he thought the financial crisis was over. He was much ridiculed for saying so: even his own staff at the National Westminster, desperately trying to cobbled together rescue packages, thought it was a bit premature. But in a sense, he was right. By the beginning of 1983, it was quite clear that the central banks of the industrial countries did not intend to allow a large bank to go bust. Of course, there is a still more dramatic possibility. Two or three giant borrowers might suddenly announce a default. If that were to happen, the central banks might find it almost impossible to prevent a rapidly spreading chain of bank collapses. Barring such a catastrophe, though, there might be some small failures, but there was going to be no rerun of the late 1920s: no International Great Crash. Some highly ingenious schemes were being worked out to salvage anyone who needed rescuing, such as a plan to allow commercial banks to rediscount (sell at discount) their Third World loans to central banks, acquiring cash but still keeping responsibility for the credit risk.

There are more substantial dangers. One is that the banks, chastened by the events of 1982, may go to the other extreme and be elaborately cautious in their lending. Or they may simply find that so large a share of resources is committed to keeping the bad debtors afloat that there is nothing left to finance more virtuous countries. Either way, the financial backwash of the crisis might mean less money for Third World investment and growth.

Some bankers, and indeed some economists, fear that in attempting to solve the crisis by pumping more money into the system, governments may spark off a new bout of international inflation. [7] The sums of money committed in the first six months after Mexico's near-collapse were certainly not enough to make this a serious worry. A meeting of the IMF interim committee in February 1983 decided to increase the resources of the Fund and of the General Agreements to Borrow (GAB) which back it up to a new total of about $100 billion. That is a big increase for the Fund, but a fleabite compared with the amounts of global debt.

There is a more disturbing version of this line of thought. It is that the countries with debt problems have actually been lent too little new money — not too much — and that nothing has been done to reduce their immediate liquidity problems. Most of the reschedulings have involved the commitment of more floating rate debt — the very form of borrowing which got the Third World debtors into trouble in the first place — and although the maturities have been longer than before, the margins on new loans have been higher than before. Rescheduling has become a highly profitable business for the banks.

The result is that many debtors will almost certainly be forced to reschedule again. Eventually, the amounts of new money which international organizations may be forced to create to deal with this liquidity crisis could indeed become alarmingly high. It may be that the situation will be rescued by a dramatic decline in international interest rates, as world inflation comes down. That would have a considerable impact. With $400 billion or so of floating rate debt, the developing countries would save about $4 billion in interest payments from each percentage point drop in interest rates.

But suppose that interest rates do not fall. Then, there will only be two other options. One will be to find some way of reducing the immediate burden of interest on Third World countries. That might involve exploring ways of indexing debt service payments to the prices of Third World exports. The only alternative is a large improvement in the debtor countries' current accounts. In other words, either the cost of debt service has to be reduced or Third World countries must be able to earn enough to meet the payments. The danger is that their efforts to reduce their debts will prolong the recession, and turn a short-term liquidity problem for the financial system into a major solvency crisis.

There are not many ways to improve a current account deficit. One is to cut back domestic demand. That may be difficult in a country like Argentina where the government has only a tenuous grip on power, although some of the borrowers − Brazil in particular − were very deft at adjusting their policies in the mid-1970s recession. Of course, there are other ways in which the current account balance may come right. There may be a shift in world prices. But that can work two ways. The collapse of the oil price early in 1983 may be splendid news for Brazil and Poland, but it means gloom for Mexico, Venezuela and Nigeria, with their economic development programme founded on the assumption of expensive oil for ever.

The big Third World borrowers seem to be doing better in early 1983 than most bystanders would have expected. The current deficit of the three largest debtors looked like falling in 1983 to less than half its 1981 level. But the most problematic question remains: what will happen to Western economic growth? One detailed set of calculations (by the US bank economist Rimmer de Vries) has reckoned that without at least a modest recovery in the OECD economies, even resolute restraint in the borrowing countries would not stop a continued rise both in the size of their current account deficits and in their foreign borrowings. Everything depends on the big export markets of the industrial West.

And on that, there are as many views as there are economists. Some believe that the US economy will rebound in 1983, fuelled by falling interest rates. Some believe that falling oil prices will trigger off a widespread revival. Some (and I am one) fear that the fragile recovery may be choked off by spreading protectionism and by a new rise in US interest rates as the tough monetary policy of the US Federal Reserve runs slap into pre-election spending and tax cuts in 1984.

If the Third World debt crisis is not resolved, it will not only be the banks which suffer. Through the mid-1970s, it was the countries of the Third World, financed by loans from the banks, which helped to reduce the impact of the world recession. If they now, in a desperate effort to balance their books, chop back their imports, depreciate their currencies, impose import controls – we will all suffer. The stability of the financial system is not a goal worth pursuing just for the peace of mind of bankers. It matters because it is so closely bound up with the smooth function of trade, of industry, of transactions among individuals, companies and countries. The events of 1982–3 were disturbingly familiar to anyone who recalled the depression of the inter-war years. Then (as Rimmer de Vries has pointed out), with world trade in a state of collapse, the default rate on Latin American bonds soared to 72 per cent (*World Financial Markets*, March 1983, p. 5).

The turmoil in the international money markets is one clear indication of the severity of the most recent international recession. But if markets cannot function properly – if borrowers cannot repay and lenders become too frightened – that will make the recession worse. In March 1983 Venezuela, which was negotiating a rescheduling, slapped a ban on imports of Scotch whisky. Thus are the jobs of Scottish Highlanders put at risk by the inability of a country on the other side of the world to repay its debts. . . .

Questions

[1] Borrowing and lending — where does the money come from?

One of the main axioms of international trade is that countries cannot consume more goods and services than they can produce through their own efforts, unless they borrow goods produced by other countries. This can be summarized as:

Total output = domestically   + goods traded for those
                     consumed goods   of another country

Total consumption = domestically   + goods obtained
                          produced goods   from another
                                                     country

It follows from this that, providing the value of goods and services it obtains from other countries does not exceed the value of output which it has produced through its own efforts, then the country is consuming to a level appropriate to its level of output. The extent to which a country consumes goods and services is an indicator of its standard of living. We can, therefore, say that with a balanced trading position a country can only raise its standard of living by raising its total domestic output.

We can now make particular interpretations of imbalances in countries' trading positions. A deficit country is consuming more than it has produced through its own efforts. It is borrowing the output of other countries' efforts and thereby obtaining a standard of living above that which it has generated for itself. It can only do this if other countries are willing to lend their output. If at some future point the lending country wants to be repaid, then the deficit country will face the massive problem of adjustment — it will have to consume fewer goods and services than it is producing in order to free a surplus to repay its past borrowing.

The position of a surplus country can be similarly regarded: it is consuming less than it has produced from its own efforts;

it could consume more and thereby raise its present standard of living but has made a conscious decision to defer consumption to a future time period. It is able to do this only insofar as there are countries willing to borrow its present output.

Table 9   World trade 1980–2

	$bn exports			$bn imports		
	1980	1981	1982	1980	1981	1982
Total developed countries	1223	1210	1145	1382	1306	1220
Total developing countries, of which:	546	539	470	443	492	454
Oil exporting nations	296	271	215	135	162	157
Other developing nations	250	268	255	308	330	297
Centrally planned economies	176	183	190	173	178	174

Source: GATT, *International Trade, 1981/2* and *1982/3*

i   *If you take all the trade surpluses away from all the trade deficits throughout the world, what figure should you finish with? (Given the sheer size of the figures there may be some margin of error.)*

ii   *Can you identify the lender and borrower countries? Is there a pattern across the world?*

iii   *Can you suggest reasons why the lender countries do not consume all the goods they could? Why do they 'save'?*

iv   *In terms of the analysis given here, explain how Third World countries repay their debts. Where does the money come from?*

v   *If the lender countries decided to recall their loans, what would the less developed countries have to do? What effect would this have upon the standard of living of their people?*

[2]   Multipliers in the Third World

If Third World countries grow by increasing their exports of particular commodities, often with the backing of investment from multinational companies, a peculiar rift develops between growth and development. It has been estimated that, in the case of Zambia, 65% of any increase in export earnings from its copper industry 'leaks' overseas in one form or another — as imports of capital and consumer goods, repatriation of profits by multinationals, etc.

Consider the following hypothetical model which incorporates these ideas:

marginal propensity to save (mps)   = 0.05
marginal propensity to be taxed (mpt) = 0.10
marginal propensity to import (mpm)   = 0.65

i   *Why does the low value for the mps accord with the Keynesian conventional wisdom concerning consumption behaviour?*

ii   *What is the multiplier for this country?*

iii   *What is the proportion of any given increase in income which gets spent on domestically produced output?*

The country starts with a GNP of $100 billion and exports contributed $20 billion to this. With help from a multinational consortium the country doubles its commodity exports.

iv   *By how much will GNP rise in percentage terms?*

v   *Explain where this increase in GNP goes — how much of it is available to expand other sectors of the economy?*

vi   *Who are the principal beneficiaries when Third World countries adopt policies of export-led growth?*

[3]   Debt servicing ratios

Figure 20 is taken from an article in the spring 1983 issue of the *Midland Bank Review*. The article, 'World recession and world debts', was written by members of the CLARE group of economists who regularly contribute highly readable articles to the *Review*.*

* A complete collection of the CLARE group articles in the *Midland Bank Review* from February 1977 to Autumn 1982 has recently been published. See *Contemporary Problems of Economic Policy: Essays from the CLARE Group*, R. C. O. Matthews and J. R. Sargent (eds), Methuen, 1983.

Figure 20 Long-term external debt* and debt service of non-oil LDCs

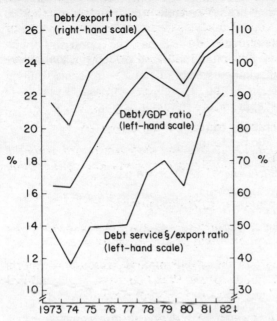

* debt with a maturity of 1 year or more contracted by public agencies or private agencies with public agency guarantees
† exports of goods and services
§ payment of interest and principal
‡ projection

i *Why have the debt servicing ratios of the non-oil LDCs increased in this way over the past decade?*

ii *What factors would cause this trend to be reversed?*

[4] Development without oil

This question takes the form of a simulation exercise based around the economy of a Third World country which has no oil reserves. The country has a population of $5\frac{1}{2}$ million and per capita GNP is $500 (UK = $5500 approx.).

The country has two major exports — some 600,000 tonnes of copper and 425,000 tonnes of zinc. It has started to develop a manufacturing base producing simple, low value semi-manufactures and finished goods. Currently it sells some 70 million units and export revenue from this source is $100 million a year.

In order to develop its industrial base the country is importing high technology capital goods and this costs $200 million annually. Its other imports are predictable — oil, some 3 million tonnes annually, and food, $1\frac{1}{2}$ million tonnes each year.

In Year 1 the appropriate trading prices are:

Copper = $1500 per tonne
Zinc   = $ 700 per tonne
Oil   = $ 217 per tonne
Food   = an average of $300 per tonne

i *Draw up a trading table and produce a figure for this country's balance of visible trade.*

In Year 2 oil prices rise by 20%, demand falling by 10% as a result.

ii *Draw up a trading position showing the effect of the oil price rise.*

The effect of the world-wide increase in oil prices is to drive the world into a recession with the result that demand for raw materials falls — reducing the country's copper exports by $150 million and zinc exports by $30 million.

iii *Again draw up the revised trading balance sheet. What is the country's overall visible trading position now?*

In the face of the economic crisis the President calls a meeting of senior ministers. Before them are a series of proposals to ease the country through the crisis:

a restriction of home demand to reduce manufactured imports
b import more high technology products through aid programmes, thereby doubling the output of manufactured goods
c borrow $232 million in the Eurodollar markets to meet external payments
d reduce the price of raw material exports in an attempt to corner a larger share of the now contracting market

iv The ministers decide to reject options a, b and d. What reasons do you think might account for their thinking?

The country now borrows $232 million through a consortium loan in the Eurodollar market at a variable rate of interest, currently 10%. The loan is repayable over 10 years.

v How much money will the country have to find to service the loan at the end of Year 2?

During Year 2 commodity prices fall by 10%, mainly due to competition among the exporters, and oil prices rise again putting a further 10% onto the country's oil import bill.

vi Re-draft the country's balance sheet at the end of the year, showing loan repayments as an import. If the country takes the option of borrowing again, how much will it need?

The OECD countries react to the world recession by raising interest rates so that the LIBOR rate averages 15% in Year 3.

vii How much in total is the country now borrowing?

viii What interest payments does it make?

ix The copper price is now $1400 per tonne – how much copper does it have to sell to meet the annual loan repayments and interest charges?

x Can you see any way out of this borrowing spiral for the country to take?

[5] Development with oil

Consider now the situation facing another developing nation. At first glance it would appear to be in a favourable position, as it is endowed with oil deposits. It has a population of 70 million and GDP per head is $450. Total exports are in the region of $10,000 million – 80% of this comes from the export of 35 million tonnes of oil annually at a price of $220 per tonne. The country is using its oil revenues to import capital goods to improve the social capital – medical facilities, education, roads, etc. – and to expand its industrial base. Putting the figures into manageable proportions, the country can spend about $142 per head of the population each year to raise living standards (how much is $142 currently in sterling terms?)

i   The country commits itself to a major education programme. How far will the money go? (Given that much of the educational material will have to be imported, it is relevant to note that the average annual cost per secondary school pupil in the UK is about $1000.)

In an attempt rapidly to increase its living standards, the country decides to borrow $20,000 million at a rate of interest of $7\frac{1}{2}\%$ over 10 years. It will service this loan by raising its oil production and exports by 25%.

ii   What are the annual costs (interest plus repayments) of this loan?

iii   What proportion of its total export revenue nows goes on debt servicing?

Two developments − the world price of oil drops by 10% and the level of interest rates rises to 15%.

iv   What is the country's export revenue now?

v   What are the annual costs of the loan now?

vi   What is the debt service : export revenue ratio now?

vii   If the country took this loan out in 1977, why might it have thought itself fairly sensible at the time?

[6]   Commodity prices 1977−81

Figure 21 shows that from October 1980 to mid-June 1981 commodity prices index fell by 17%.

i   Given that prices fall when either supply or demand for products experiences a significant change, suggest reasons for this substantial fall.

ii   In what ways would Third World countries possibly benefit and suffer from the trends shown in the figure?

Figure 21 Commodity prices (US $ index)

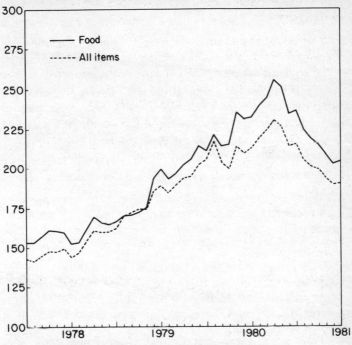

Source: *Midland Bank Review*, Autumn/Winter 1981

[7] Trade deficits and inflation

This exercise is designed to show how Third World countries
with large deficits and borrowing requirements benefited from
high of world inflation in the early 1970s. Throughout
this model we use the notion of a 'consumer unit' – this is
because we need a standard physical measure of internationally
traded goods. We simplify in the exercise by assuming that the
two countries only trade in consumer goods. A consumer unit
could be = one pen = $\frac{1}{2}$% of a refrigerator = 5 bars of
chocolate = etc. It is a standard unit. We are going to observe
the relationship between two countries in Year 1.

Country A has a balance of trade surplus of $1 million. It
derived the surplus because its domestic output in Year 1 was

10 million consumer units but it only consumed 9 million itself — the remainder were sold for $1 each on world markets.

i Country B has a balance of trade deficit; as there are only two countries in this model, what is B's deficit and assuming its domestic output for the year to be 9 million units, how did B's deficit occur?

Country B will have to finance its deficit by borrowing the money officially from Country A. Now let a year pass in which prices rise by 10% throughout the world. At the end of the year A asks B to repay loans made to finance its trade deficit. Country A now seeks to spend the $1 million.

ii How many consumer units will Country A now be able to buy?

iii In order to raise the money to repay the loan, B has to sell some of its domestic output to the residents of A. How many consumer units does B have to sell to raise $1 million?

In Year 1 Country A 'underconsumed' by 1 million units but when it came to consume its surplus in Year 2 discovered that it could only claim 909,000 — it has in effect lost 91,000 consumer units. In Year 1 Country B overconsumed by 1 million units but when it came to repay them in Year 2 only had to repay 909,000 — effectively gaining the 91,000 units. The analysis clearly shows that the real value of trading surpluses and deficits can be eroded by inflation.

As in all borrowing and lending, an unexpected increase in prices benefits borrowers at the expense of lenders — real income is transferred from lenders to borrowers. Thus during times of high inflation there was a substantial, if inadvertent, real income transfer towards less developed nations.

iv So what was the effect on the LDCs of the concerted effort by the OECD countries in the late 1970s/early 1980s to 'rid the world of the curse of inflation'?

Further reading

The most readable and one of the most astute sources on the Third World debt problem is *World Financial Markets*, published monthly by the Morgan Guaranty Trust Company of New York and available free from the Purchasing Department, Morgan Guaranty Trust Company, P.O. Box 161, Morgan House, 1 Angel Court, London EC2R 7AE. The annual report of the Bank for International Settlements in Basle, Switzerland is more massively comprehensive and often the first public confirmation of advancing trouble.

6 Local authority rates – why have they survived?

President Reagan's right-wing government in the United States has gone to some lengths to try to hand power back to the individual states. It is a government committed to decentralization. By contrast, Mrs Thatcher's government has done no such thing. In its desire to control the expenditure of local authorities, it has diminished their authority and greatly increased the power of central government.

Behind the tangled financial relations of central and local government – which are the subject of this chapter – lies a political battle. Governments always tend to make polite noises about the importance of local democracy. But when it comes to the crunch, the desire to influence or control local authority spending is apt to override politeness.

Mrs Thatcher originally came to power at a late stage in one of the periodic crises which erupt in relations between the authorities and Westminster. The inflation of the 1970s created an outburst of complaints about rates. Rates did not, in fact, rise faster than retail prices or incomes for most of the period, but people who remembered their rate demands of previous years found that hard to believe. So central government – first under Mr Callaghan and then under Mrs Thatcher – became anxious to check the rise in the one tax which was outside their control.

At first, the focus of attention was on rates themselves. A lot of very old ground was ploughed up. Could they be scrapped? If so, what should replace them? Then, as public expenditure became more of a political issue, the emphasis shifted to attempts to influence what local authorities spent.

By the time Michael Heseltine left the Department of the Environment in January 1983 – and battered borough treasurers heaved a sigh of relief – the crisis had more or less resolved itself. Inflation had fallen – and so had the increases in rates. Local authority spending had fallen back sharply: although the fall was almost entirely the result of cuts in capital spending, and particularly in new council house building. No progress had been made in transferring the most labour-intensive functions of local government to the private sector: and so there had been no great decline in current spending, the bulk of which consisted of wages and salaries. Still, in real terms, current spending had at least paused in its apparently inexorable rise.

This might look like success. But even as local authorities struck rates averaging a modest 7 per cent up on the previous year in 1983, it was clear that the situation was not really sustainable. Once expenditure begins to rise again, observers reflected, one of three outcomes is probable. Either local authorities will raise the rates, and there will be a new discussion of alternative sources of local revenue. Or the central government – to avoid a rise in the rates – will increase the size of the grant it pays to top up local income, in which case the extent to which local authority voters pay for their own spending will diminish. Or the central government will transfer some services out of the hands of local authorities, in which case local autonomy will be further eroded.

The problem has two roots. First, the revenues of local authorities are inadequate and inappropriate for them to finance the services which they – and central government – would like to see provided. Rates raise an enormous amount of money. But the way in which they are levied makes it extremely difficult to increase their yield. There is a clear need either to supplement (or replace) them with some other tax, or to find another way of financing some of the services they pay for.

Secondly, the whole concept of local democracy has been undermined by the tangled lines of responsibility between central and local government. Domestic ratepayers – those who actually elect local authorities – now pay for no more than about 13 per cent of all rate fund expenditure. At the same time, a great deal of local authority spending is effectively dictated by central government. So we have a situation where local authorities, elected by people who do not finance them, are financing spending over which they do not have full control. That is not a recipe for effective local democracy.

To see these two strands of the problem more clearly, it might be worth taking them one by one. First, the inadequacy of the financial base. The bulk of local authorities' own revenues come from rates, a property tax levied not just on domestic dwellings but on industrial and commercial properties as well. The astonishing thing about rates is their durability. They have survived repeated committees of inquiry into local taxation, a firm commitment in the 1974 Conservative election manifesto to abolish them, and a rather more watery promise in the 1979 manifesto. In a Green Paper in December 1981 (Alternatives to Domestic Rates, Cmnd 8449) the Conservative government declared itself 'committed to the reform of the domestic rating system'. Yet rates have survived.

They survive because they raise a great deal of money. Their total yield is almost as large as the yield from Value Added Tax (see Table 10). More than half the total comes from non-domestic ratepayers. There are three reasons why rates do not work well. First, they are not assessed on capital values, but on the income a property might earn if it were rented out. This makes some sense with industrial and commercial property, but none at all with domestic dwellings, for which a free market in rentals is virtually extinct. When domestic property was last revalued for rating purposes (to discover how relative

Table 10 Yield from major taxes, rates and National Insurance contributions, 1982–3

	£ billion
Income tax	30.2
National Insurance contributions	18.6
Value Added Tax	13.9
Oil duties	5.2
Corporation tax	5.5
Tobacco	3.5
Spirits, beer, wine and perry	3.0
Local authority rates	12.3
of which approximately:	
Non-domestic rates	7.0
Domestic rates	5.3

Source: Financial Statement and Budget Report 1983–4, and Treasury estimates

rentals had moved) it was calculated that fewer than 2 per cent of privately owned dwellings were let at rents which could be used as a benchmark for rates. In other words, the taxable value of 98 per cent of dwellings was based on inferences from 2 per cent of dwellings (Malcolm Crawford and Diane Dawson, 'Are rates the right tax for local government?', *Lloyds Bank Review*, July 1982, pp. 15–35). [1]

That is nutty enough. But worse is the fact that revaluations have been repeatedly postponed – most recently, the revaluation due in 1982 was called off. Each time there is a revaluation, some people's rate bills leap (because their area has become fashionable) and others' fall. The losers complain more loudly than the winners rejoice. So older, urban properties remain by general agreement over-rated, while newer, suburban dwellings escape reasonably lightly.

A second difficulty is that rates, as a tax on property, suffer from the drawbacks of other wealth taxes: the bill bears little relationship to ability to pay. By and large, rich people tend to live in properties with high rates and poor people in properties with low rates. But there are many exceptions. And everyone knows of a family with husband, wife and three teenage children all at work who live next door to a little old pensioner with precisely the same rates bill. [2, 3]

This criticism has been mitigated by the introduction of rate rebates. They are taken up by roughly 70 per cent of the households which are eligible for them. But rate rebates are means-tested, and like all means-tested benefits they leave a band of fairly poor families at a point where each additional pound of income earned is largely or totally offset by a loss of income from the state. The December 1981 Green Paper pointed out that the families paying the highest proportion of their income in rates were those on £100 a week, who paid 4 per cent. Thereafter the proportion fell, and the average is just over 2 per cent.

A third difficulty with rates is their impact on non-domestic property from which, in 1980–81, 57 per cent of the net yield of rates was raised. About three-quarters of non-domestic rates are paid by companies. With the collapse of company profits and the consequent decline in the yield from corporation tax, rates have almost become a larger tax burden on companies than corporation tax. For many individual businesses, rates now constitute their biggest single tax.

Businesses feel bitterness with more justification than domestic ratepayers. Of course, businesses do not end up footing the bill for the tax: only individuals can do that, and often individuals who live in different local authorities. But businesses enjoy directly far fewer services from local authorities than individuals – and they have not, since 1969, had a vote. They may lobby, and lobby very effectively (they have the ultimate sanction of leaving an area and taking jobs with them). But it cannot be healthy that more than half of local authority rate income should come from the unenfranchized. [4]

True, rates do not seem to be a very large part of company costs. One cannot be sure: the most recent firm figures are way back in the 1968 Census of Production, and they suggest that even in retailing, by far the most heavily rated part of the private sector, rates only account for $4\frac{1}{2}$ per cent of net output. In every other private sector activity, rates (in 1968) were less than 2 per cent of net output.

But one of the curiosities about rates is that the fuss people make about them is out of proportion to the burden they impose. Most people would never guess that net rates took less than $2\frac{1}{2}$ per cent of their income (and always have done – see Table 11); most traders would never guess that rates were roughly as burdensome as their electricity bill. My own guess is that the outcry over rates is made much worse by the fact that the sum is demanded annually, and each year's bill shows a figure which can be readily compared with last year's bill. How many of us have the foggiest notion what we paid in income tax last year? Or in Value Added Tax? Yet our contribution to both taxes was undoubtedly much larger than our rates payment.

Plenty of alternatives to rates have been proposed. Most of them have considerable drawbacks. Before considering them, though, it might be worth seeing the way in which the inflexibility of the rate base impinges on the other major problems of local authority finance: the hopeless entanglement of financial accountability and the responsibility for policy. To understand the tangle it is necessary to have at least a brief glance at the way local authorities' budgets are organized.

Table 11 Rates and income

	Net domestic rate as % of personal disposable income
1938/39	2.71
1952/53	1.94
1955/56	1.92
1958	2.16
1959	2.15
1960	2.11
1961	2.11
1962	2.21
1963	2.33
1964	2.45
1965	2.52
1966	2.57
1967	2.57
1968	2.48
1969	2.46
1970	2.38
1971	2.47
1972	2.45
1973	2.36
1974	2.01
1975	2.07
1976	2.09
1977	2.15
1978	2.07
1979	2.07
1980*	2.22

* estimate

Source: Christopher Foster, 'How to arrest the decline of local government', *Public Money*, June 1981

Local authorities spent a total of £29 billion in 1980–81. Only £4.4 billion of that was capital expenditure, while nearly £13 billion represented staffing costs. Of local authority income, 26 per cent came from the rates, and 14 per cent from charges for services, including rents for council houses; far and away the biggest single chunk — 46 per cent — came from government grants (see Figure 22).

It is the form taken by these central government grants which have been the focus for public debate on the control of local government spending. The problem is this. The central government can limit the capital spending of local authorities very closely, because they need its permission to borrow. That is reasonable enough: everyone knows that if an authority went bust, the central government would bail it out, and authorities can therefore borrow at interest rates close to (or even below) the rate paid by the central government. If the central government is going to guarantee local authority debt, it must control the quantity of that debt. Besides, the local authorities are competing for much the same pool of funds as central government.

But over the total of local authority current spending, central government has no such precise control. And quite right, too, if local democracy is to have any meaning. For one of the main justifications for the existence of local authorities is surely that different communities have different spending priorities, and that it may be healthier for a democracy to decentralize power. The corollary of true decentralization,

Figure 22 All local authority income by source

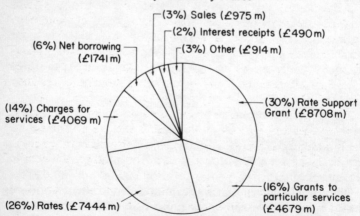

Source: *Local Government Financial Statistics England and Wales 1980/81*, Department of the Environment, HMSO, 1982

however, is inevitably some lack of control over expenditure by the centre.

Central government constantly regrets this lack of control. The authorities argue that the proper interest of the central government is in the size of the grant it gives them. Spending financed from the rates should be of no concern, because it does not influence aggregate demand and merely substitutes public goods for private goods by local choice. There is some justice in their claim; although to the extent that rate-financed expenditure substitutes public consumption for private saving, it does have an impact on aggregate demand.

But the more fundamental problem is that central government simply does not trust the authorities to spend responsibly. And why should they? The turnout at local elections is frequently less than a third of the electorate. The voters usually vote on national issues, rather than local ones. The two-party system ensures that the same group of councillors may sit in the town hall year after year. Local elections are infrequent. Local council officials have frequently a natural interest in expanding spending: more chaps in the planning department increases the self-esteem of the Planning Officer. And as we have already seen, the fact that the domestic ratepayer stumps up one pound in eight of rate fund expenditure makes local authority spending a marvellous buy. [5]

All that central government has been able to do about these built-in incentives to spend is to chop back the grant it makes to the authorities. But there are two problems with that. First, the grant was never intended as a way of controlling spending. And second, if a local authority's grant is cut, it may turn to the rates to replace lost revenue — and precipitate a shoal of letters onto the desk of the Secretary of State for the Environment. [6]

The central government's main weapon of control over the current spending of local authorities is the grant it makes to top up their rates income. As always, when a piece of machinery designed for one purpose is used for another, the results are chaotic.

The original purpose of the central government grant to local authorities was to balance out differences in resources and in needs. One of the drawbacks to rates is that their basis — rateable values — vary far more around the country than

133

do incomes. So the rate base differs considerably, and the central government has always accepted a responsibility to make a grant, financed out of national taxes, to equalize the amount which an extra penny on the rates would raise in any authority.

Balancing resources is easier than balancing needs. A second purpose of the central government grant has been to allow for the fact that some authorities need more money to provide the same level of service for each citizen as others. Some authorities have a disproportionately old population: they need more money to allow for the extra costs of personal social services. Some have a disproportionately large number of roads to maintain, relative to the size of their total population: they need extra money to keep up their highways.

It sounds simple enough. But measuring 'need' is always a slippery business. Per head of their populations, local authorities spend very much the same amount on the police, and on the fire brigade. They spend wildly differing amounts on personal social services (meals on wheels, home helps – that sort of thing). A study of the differences in 1976–7 found that spending ranged from £9.15 a head in Solihull up to £61.24 a head in Tower Hamlets, with the wealthier shire countries clustered between £10 and £20, and the Inner London boroughs averaging nearly £50 a head (C. Foster, R. A. Jackman and M. Perlman, *Local Government Finance in a Unitary State*, Allen & Unwin, 1980).

What is one to make of that? It is probably true that there are many more poor and elderly people in inner London than in the shire counties. But is that the whole story? Do the shire counties provide fewer personal social services than their populations 'need'? Or do the London boroughs provide more? And where does a government which wants to try to finance the same basic level of provision everywhere eventually strike a balance?

When the Conservative administration first came to power in 1979, it was worried that the way in which the grant was being assessed measured 'needs' in a way which actually encouraged local authorities to spend more. Because the government was anxious to restrain local authority spending, it set to work to change the way the central government's grant was worked out. There had been moves to change it before, recommended by the Layfield Committee which reported on local government finance in 1976 and developed by Mr Callaghan's Labour Government, but shelved in the face of opposition from the local authorities.

Under the old system, the central government Rate Support Grant had two main parts: the 'resources' element, and a much larger 'needs' element. Needs were worked out under a complicated formula based on what each authority had spent last year and on a number of indicators such as the length of roads, or the numbers of old people or school pupils. In theory, it provided an objective measure of need; in practice, it was highly subjective: by raising the weighting for one factor or another, the government of the day could channel extra money to authorities of its own political persuasion. The formula also had a built-in tendency to reward big spenders: the more an authority spent, the greater its 'need' was measured to be in subsequent years.

So in a bill of great length and enormous complexity (The Local Government, Planning and Land Act, 1980), the Thatcher government changed the basis for grant calculations to a unitary or block grant. Gone was the old complicated formula; in its place was a new and even more complicated formula. The main change, though, was an important one: the concept of 'need' as something which could be determined by what had been spent in the past has gone. In its place is the centralist idea of a 'right' level for local spending, which the government uses the grant machinery to prescribe.

This 'right' level is known as 'grant related expenditure' or GRE. (Mr Heseltine used to pronounce it Greer, as in Germaine.) It is calculated by looking at the size of groups in the population which might need particular services – a system which has resulted in a few local authorities receiving grant to cover the cost of services which they have never provided. The theory behind the new system, though, is that if every local authority spent exactly its grant related expenditure – the amount the government judges it 'needs' to spend – then every authority in the country could levy the same rate poundage, in terms of pence in the pound. This is backed up with a penalty, which reduces the grant of some authorities as they overspend. [7]

135

It is an elegant concept. But even before it had a chance to be applied in a round of grant negotiations, Mr Heseltine had realized that the new unitary grant would not deliver the spending cuts he wanted in time. Indeed, it soon became clear that in the short run the new machinery might well cause an increase in spending. For one thing, some authorities would find they had been spending less than their GRE and jack up their budgets, while others, who had been spending more than their GREs, would continue to sin. So on top of its elaborate new structure, the government had to superimpose crude spending targets, under which all authorities, regardless of their GRE, were ordered to cut their spending on pain of losing part of their grant. The result was some lunatic situations. Gillingham, in Kent, found itself in 1983–4 with a spending target only half its GRE – only half, in other words, the sum which the government itself calculated that Gillingham 'needed' to spend. It is, say the authorities, the end of local democracy. [8]

And so it may well turn out to be, without some reform in the financial relations between central and local government. But reform in isolation will provide no solutions. One of the insights in Professor Alan Day's note of reservation to the Layfield report was 'causation [ran] from political aims and policies to financial mechanisms, rather than in the opposite direction from financial mechanisms to political aims and policies. It is desirable', Professor Day continued, 'to set up financial mechanisms which are most likely to serve the kinds of political aims which can be foreseen. . . . The establishment of financial mechanisms which do not accord with the political will of the government can be of little benefit in maintaining local autonomy' ('Local government finance', Report of a Committee of Enquiry under Frank Layfield, Cmnd 6453, May 1976, HMSO, pp. 306–7).

In other words, it would be quite pointless to provide local authorities with some generous new source of funds – from a local income tax, for instance – if central government did not also want local authorities to enjoy a great degree of control over their expenditure.

The crux of the problem at the moment is that the lines of responsibility are tangled. Governments to a large extent dictate what local authorities must spend. How much, one cannot be sure — but one way and another, central government probably influences about three-quarters of an average authority's spending. After all, it is in Whitehall that teachers' salaries are negotiated (and that alone accounts for a quarter of local authority current spending). It is in Whitehall that the school leaving age is set, that minimum standards for housing are devised, that decisions are taken to allow geriatric wards to be closed down and old people to be turfed out into 'community care'. There are other influences on spending which are less direct: all those circulars, for instance, which do not have the force of directives but which urge local authorities to make this item or that a matter of priority in their budgets. Sites for gypsies, better day-care for under fives, sports centres, clubs for the elderly: all sorts of ministerial daydreams tend to end up as a Whitehall circular to local authorities.

Meanwhile the inadequacy of local taxation means that anything which causes local spending to rise has to be financed by the central government. The long-term upward pressure on local authority spending has inevitably been very strong. It is carried along by demography (more old people mean more spending on social services), by a desire to improve standards (more nursery schools mean spending from the educational budget), and by the pressure of local authority trade unions (because local authority services are highly labour intensive, their cost frequently rises more rapidly than prices in the economy as a whole). [9]

But a rise in the rates to pay for such increases in expenditure means nasty letters to the Secretary of State for the Environment. So the natural temptation for any government has been to remove services from local control — or to raise the size of the central government grant. That has created a vicious circle. The larger the grant relative to rates, the larger increase in rates is required to offset any reduction in grant. It is a question of arithmetic.

To swap rates for another tax — or to supplement them with some local source of finance — might be a partial solution. Certainly, it is hard to see how the proportion of central government grant to local authorities can be permanently restrained without a more elastic financial base. A point repeatedly made in the massive study of local authority finance, by Professor Christopher Foster and his two colleagues (see p. 134), is that the 'addiction to grant' of local authorities is the principle threat to local control over local spending. And there is no way that non-domestic rates can be abolished − as they certainly ought to be − without some new source of income.

But what alternatives are there really to rates? There have been lots of ingenious suggestions. There are problems with all of them. A local sales tax? Mrs Thatcher persists in preferring that option: but it would create a wonderful new industry, smuggling goods from authorities with high taxes to those with low. A local profits tax? Accountants would have a field day with transfer pricing between Croydon and Camden. A local payroll tax? That would be a tax on those who worked in an area, rather than those who lived there and enjoyed its services. The only serious option is a local income tax.

Local income tax was picked out by the Layfield Committee in its report. The Committee examined the option in some detail, and argued the case for a tax built into the PAYE system, side by side with national income tax and collected by the Inland Revenue. It would undoubtedly have advantages. Because income varies less around the country than rateable values, it would greatly reduce the need for central government to try to equalize resources among authorities. And it would be more progressive than rates − although poorer people who currently draw rate rebates might find themselves paying more.

There would inevitably be some problems. At the moment, income tax is collected on the basis of where people work, and where their company's head office is located. This difficulty − like almost every other difficulty relating to income tax − is probably exaggerated and in any case will become easier once tax collection is finally tranferred to computer. Meanwhile, official enthusiasm for local income tax is negligible, and we soldier on with rates.

An even more controversial option is to extend charging. In the past, local authorities have not adopted any sort of coherent policy towards charges. They raise the equivalent of about a quarter of their current expenditure from charges. But more than half of that comes solely from council house rents. There are large and illogical variations in the extent to which other services cover their costs from charges. The Layfield Report found that car parking facilities covered 60 per cent of their costs; homes for the elderly 34 per cent; libraries, museums and art galleries, 5 per cent; refuse collection, 4 per cent. Not much sign of a unifying theory behind all that.

There is one respect in which the argument in favour of charging is absolutely clear-cut. If non-domestic rates were abolished, there would be a good case for charging businesses for the services with which local authorities provide them, wherever it was economic to do so. But in other respects, the arguments are more complex. [10]

There is a good case for providing some local authority services for free. They are the services which economists describe as 'public goods'. In a nutshell, they are those goods − and services − which private producers will not provide efficiently. They have two particular characteristics which distinguish them from private goods. First, it is impossible to charge individual consumers for the public goods which they consume. Street cleaning is one obvious example; prison is another. Second, it is possible for people to consume more of a public good without adding to the costs of providing it. Think of street lighting, or the view of St Paul's Cathedral.

Those examples are ones in which everyone would agree. But others are more difficult. Is education a public good? If education only increases the earning power and the happiness of a particular individual, then it is a private good and might logically bear a charge. But if education improves the working of a democracy, or makes us all happier and richer, then it is a public good and it is logical to provide it for free. To determine what is a particular good, it may be necessary first to decide who benefits from it − and that may be a political, rather than a factual question.

With a great many of the services which local authorities provide, it is possible to argue that they are really not public goods. The benefits of council housing, or meals on wheels, or public libraries, or refuse collection accrue largely or entirely to individual consumers. The usual reason why local authorities do not charge an economic price for providing them is that they are a form of redistribution: of transferring money from the better off to the poor.

But the problem with this sort of redistribution is that it leaves the consumer with little choice; and it makes it impossible to discover where the consumer's true preferences lie. Given the money it costs to provide meals on wheels, old ladies might prefer to buy an evening out at Raymond's Revuebar. To charge for some of the services which local authorities provide would not necessarily rule out redistribution, only paternalism. But it would require either a radical change in the taxation system − in the form of some sort of negative income tax − or a voucher system.

Vouchers have generally been considered in relation to education. They might work like this. People would be given vouchers entitling them to so much education − and if they wanted to send their children to a particular school, they would be free to top up the cost from their own pocket. The system would ensure a minimum standard of education for everyone, but allow people who placed a high priority on education to choose something better than the minimum. [11]

There is undoubtedly a case for trying to put local authority charging on a more coherent basis. One study (*Service Provision and Pricing in Local Government: Studies in Local Environment Services*, HMSO, November 1981) of charging for environmental services − like refuse collection − found that the reason why local authorities so often charged less than the full cost of providing the service was not usually any sophisticated concern about public goods or even redistribution; it was simply that they miscalculated the real cost of the capital assets − refuse lorries or whatever − involved, and they had underestimated what the market would be willing to pay. The correct policy with services of this sort might be to charge them at full cost − unless there are good reasons to the contrary.

To extend charging for local authority services would not necessarily reduce public spending. To some extent, it would simply alter the channels through which central government pays for local services: to the social security system, perhaps, or to negative income tax or to bearing the cost of issuing vouchers. At the same time, it would diminish the direct leverage which the grant gives central government on local authority spending. Would any government be willing to accept that? [12]

In any case, a more flexible source of local authority finance is only half of the problem. The other half is to clarify the responsibility for spending local authority budgets. One ingenious solution put forward by Professor Alan Day in his dissenting note is a system under which central government lays down and finances a minimum level of services; anything over and above that would be financed by individual local authorities, as they chose. There are, however, two important drawbacks to such a solution. One is that an acceptable minimum level of most services might not be much lower than what is already being provided. There might be very little room left for local authority discretion.

The second hitch is the familiar problem of measuring the quality of a service. How would the minimum standard be defined? In terms of the numbers employed? The amount of money spent? Or in terms of output: of children passing O-levels, of tons of refuse collected, of library books borrowed? There are difficulties with both techniques: and they are not very different from the problems which have made the new block grant such a nightmare to administer.

If one asks what is most likely to happen − as opposed to what ought to happen − the immediate prospect after the 1983 General Election is that the new Conservative government will abandon its attempts to nudge local authorities into restraint. Instead, Patrick Jenkin, the new Environment secretary, is proposing a crude ceiling on rate increases by big spenders − with reserve powers to impose ceilings on the rate increases of all authorities. This is a solution of despair. If his proposals become law, they will bring in their wake a greater degree of central control over spending than any government has yet been willing to contemplate.

Questions

[1] Taxation of housing – present system (owner-occupied)

The present system of taxation of housing in the UK defies all economic logic. The income tax system allows home owners who are buying with a mortgage to offset mortgage interest against tax. This tax relief, which goes mainly to the better-off, is estimated to be in the region of £2 billion annually, and makes a house a much more attractive investment than industrial shares.

Consider the following example:

A householder buys a 3-bedroomed house for £28,000 by placing a deposit of £3,000 and obtaining a building society mortgage for £25,000. At a mortgage interest rate of 10% over 20 years the person will pay £1,687 each year to the building society in interest payments. (Given the way building societies charge interest this will be an average figure and the exact nature of the payments is slightly different following tax changes introduced in 1983.)

i If the householder was paying tax at the standard rate of 30p in the £, how much tax will now be saved by setting the interest off against income tax?

The local authority in which this house is situated assesses its rateable value at £167 and levies a rate of 183p in the £.

ii How much domestic rate will this householder pay?

iii What is the householder's net payment to government as 'housing tax'?

iv As you move up the income scale what happens to the transfer of income from government to householder?

v This system can be seen as reducing the opportunity cost of buying a home – explain with the aid of diagrams the effect this is likely to have on housing prices.

If you buy an antique piece of furniture, renovate it and sell it for a much higher price, you are liable for what is called Capital Gains Tax. You can renovate a house with a grant from your local council, sell it some years after at a vast profit — and owner-occupied houses are exempt from Capital Gains Tax.

[2] Taxation of housing — a return to the past?

Until 1963 the basis for housing taxation in the UK was the Schedule A tax system developed in Lloyd George's 1909 Budget. Under this system a house was regarded as an asset which generated income: you can rent it out, but if you own it and live in it you are saving the income you would otherwise have spent renting something similar. The notional income was, therefore, taxed. Mortgage interest payments and maintenance costs were set against the tax liability and the householder was taxed on net income.

Thus in the previous example, a 3-bedroomed Victorian house might be seen as generating a Schedule A income of £3000 pa — with mortgage interest payments at £1687 and maintenance costs around £300, the tax payment would be £300 at the standard rate of tax.

i   *Schedule A taxation of housing operated through the income tax system. Was it, therefore, capable of being a progressive tax?*

There are proposals to reform the housing taxation system by the introduction of a Schedule A tax levied on the capital values of houses instead of on the imputed rental income.

> 'The first elements of the reform of the market for housing must be restoration of sound economic principles by restoring Schedule A taxation, the abolition or reduction of the mortgage interest tax offset and the application of capital gains taxation to housing.'
>
> Alan Maynard, 'The economics of housing', in
> D. Gowland (ed.), *Modern Economic Analysis*,
> Butterworth, 1982

ii   *Who would oppose such a system and why?*

[3] Rates as a regressive form of taxation

Figure 23 shows the proportions of gross household income paid in the form of direct and indirect taxes in 1980 by ten income groups in the UK.

Figure 23   Direct and indirect taxes as a per cent of gross household income, 1980

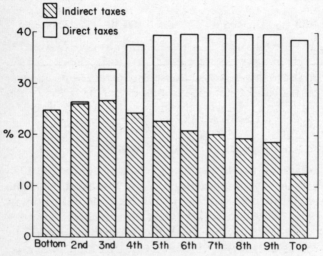

Source: *Lloyds Bank Review*, July 1982, p. 21

i   Give definitions of a direct and indirect tax. Direct taxes are usually said to be progressive − what does this mean?

ii   To what extent does the evidence in Figure 23 confirm the belief that UK indirect taxes are regressive in their effect?

iii   From the evidence in Table 12 (p. 145) which is the most regressive tax in the UK?

iv   Why is it that rates as a percentage of disposable income per household fall as income rises?

[4] Franchise problems

'Taxation without representation is tyranny' was the watchword of the American Revolution.

To what extent is this an appropriate phrase to describe the present rating system in the UK?

144

Table 12 Indirect taxes as a per cent of disposable income per household, 1980

Quintile groups of households	Domestic rates	VAT	Other indirect taxes	Total indirect taxes
Bottom fifth	3.7–6.9[1]	5.4	13.2	23.0–25.6
Next fifth	4.9–5.2[1]	7.4	15.6	28.0–28.3
Middle fifth	3.8–3.9[1]	7.5	15.1	26.4–26.5
Next fifth	3.2	7.4	14.1	24.7
Top fifth	2.5	7.1	12.3	21.9

[1] The ranges shown for the burden of rates reflect alternative treatments of rates paid by supplementary benefit households. See *Economic Trends*, No. 339, January 1982.

Source: *Lloyds Bank Review*, July 1982, p. 21

[5] Paying for local authority expenditure

The chapter says that domestic ratepayers only pay about 13% of the cost of local authority provision. The majority of the cost *is* paid by them but in the confused combination of income tax, VAT, etc. which makes up central government revenue from which grants to local authorities are made. The remainder of the burden which is borne by commercial ratepayers is ultimately paid by the domestic ratepayer in that part of final goods' prices which carry companies' rate costs. The argument is that ratepayers are only aware of the direct payment through the annual rates bill.

If they stopped to think about it ratepayers would recognize the hidden costs – for example, a household with two secondary school age children may be paying rates of £300 a year. The local authority is likely to spend £1000 per secondary school pupil on education costs.

i *Economists employ marginal utility theory to explain how consumers allocate their income to maximize satisfaction. What does marginal utility theory predict consumers will do if they think the cost of a product to them is only 20% of its true cost?*

ii *Can you think of areas where ratepayers might 'over-consume' because of this?*

[6] Rates and grants

An imaginary local authority has a total expenditure of £1000 million annually. This is financed:

   60% grants from central government
   30% from rates
   10% charges for services

The product of a penny rate in this authority yields £$\frac{1}{2}$ million.

i What will the rate poundage be in this case?

The council is now told that the central government proposes to reduce its grants by 5%.

ii How much will the local authority lose as a consequence of this?

iii What options are open to the local authority to restore balance to its budget?

iv Should the authority choose to raise the deficit from the rates, what percentage increase in the rates will be necessary?

v A local ratepayers association, probably with close affiliations to a representative organization of local businesses, makes the following accusation in the local press:

> *In a year when inflation has only gone up by 10%, the Council has increased rates by 30%.*

Draw up a 50-word press release on the part of the Council, explaining why rates had to rise by so much.

[7] Increasing the rates

Figure 24 shows how one local authority (Avon County) sought to explain the increase in rates for 1983–4 to its ratepayers. This council estimates that increasing the rates by 1p raises £589,000.

i How does the local authority calculate the 'penny rate product'?

ii What would cause the penny rate product to rise?

Figure 24 Avon County Council and your rates

The County Council has issued a precept of 168p in the £ for the 1983/84 financial year. This compares with a precept of 156p for 1982/83. The increase amounts to 12p or 7·7%.

Why the County Rate has increased

After allowing for a modest increase in rateable values, the reasons for the 12p in the £ increase are as follows:

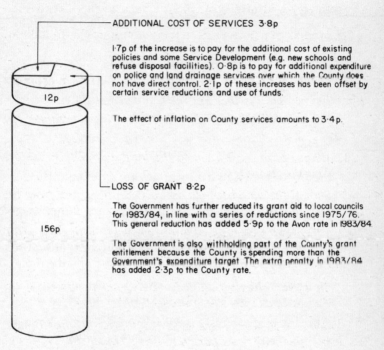

ADDITIONAL COST OF SERVICES 3·8p

1·7p of the increase is to pay for the additional cost of existing policies and some Service Development (e.g. new schools and refuse disposal facilities). 0·8p is to pay for additional expenditure on police and land drainage services over which the County does not have direct control. 2·1p of these increases has been offset by certain service reductions and use of funds.

The effect of inflation on County services amounts to 3·4p.

LOSS OF GRANT 8·2p

The Government has further reduced its grant aid to local councils for 1983/84, in line with a series of reductions since 1975/76. This general reduction has added 5·9p to the Avon rate in 1983/84.

The Government is also withholding part of the County's grant entitlement because the County is spending more than the Government's expenditure target. The extra penalty in 1983/84 has added 2·3p to the County rate.

iii *Explain how the additional cost of services rose by the product of a 3.8p rate.*

iv *By roughly how much did Avon lose grants from the central government? What reasons are given for this?*

[8] Allocative efficiency

In economics allocative efficiency measures the way in which scarce resources are shared out among the production of various

147

goods and services which the economy produces. Resources are said to be allocated efficiently when it is not possible to use them any differently without making someone worse off. This criterion of efficiency is called the Pareto criterion, after the Italian economist Vilfredo Pareto.

Suppose the functions of local government are taken over increasingly by central government departments. Then the acceptable level of provision of services will be centrally determined.

i   *Why might such a system of provision be subject to allocative inefficiency?*

ii   *What evidence is there in the chapter that the new GRE system is creating such inefficiencies?*

iii   *Why might charging for services by preferable?*

[9]   Income elasticity and local authority expenditure

The expenditure of local authorities is peculiar in that there will be demands for it to increase in times when the community's income is rising and also when it is falling. It is as if local authority provision embraces both inferior goods and luxury goods.

i   *Use the expression for income elasticity of demand to show what is meant by the terms 'inferior' and 'luxury' goods.*

ii   *Use the list in question 12, 'Why tax houses anyway' (page 151), to identify areas of local authority spending which might have to rise as community income falls.*

iii   *In which areas of local authority expenditure are the rate-paying public likely to demand increases at a time when community income is rising?*

[10]   Charging for local authority services

One suggested way of covering some local authority expenditure is to charge the user for the service. Such an option may sound very simple but it raises problems which apply to the charges levied by public sector industries generally.

i Consider a local authority sports complex which cost £2½ million to build and has estimated running costs of £¼ million annually. Prepare a policy paper for presentation to the Council's Finance and General Purposes Committee suggesting methods of charging for the services of the sports centre in a way that will cover costs.

ii Suppose you had to devise a way to charge for use of a library. What alternatives are there to charging the same fee for each book borrowed?

iii Does the decision to charge by a local authority mean that the good in question is no longer a public good?

[11] Voucher system in education

The present system of educational provision in this country is a tax and transfer system − central and local government raise taxes to pay for schools and then make the facilities available to all without direct charge. It is also a system of direct public provision − the state both controls and provides education.

Education is a peculiar product. Rather like car seat belts the law makes you consume it; unlike car seat belts it gives you no choice as to where you obtain supplies. Unless you are prepared to pay for private education you are told to report for education at a certain neighbourhood school run by the government. The 1981 Education Act gives some element of parental choice, but this is always choice between like and like. A great deal of public debate centres on 'good' and 'bad' schools, but the rather depressing fact about the vast majority of schools, both private and state, is their 'sameness' − same subjects, same hours, same pattern of working day, same organization, same rules and codes of behaviour.

A market economy relies upon consumer choice − consumers use their spending power to influence producers to make available goods and services which yield maximum satisfaction to consumers. A voucher system is seen as a way of allocating resources in education more efficiently − that is, to provide a pattern of education which makes available types of schools which meet the diverse requirements of all groups in society. If we are given the right to choose between countless types of knickers, why no choice over such an important product as schools?

One possibility if a voucher system were introduced would be that parents continue to pay taxes and rates but when their children reach school age they would not be told where the education would take place. Instead they would receive a voucher entitling the child to a year's education. They would present the voucher and the child at a school of their choice; the school would then hand the voucher to the government which would pay over the cash. Each school would then make its payments for staff, books, facilities, etc. out of the revenue derived. Schools would also have a choice over what 'factor mix' to employ, unlike the present system where local authorities dictate staff : pupil ratios, levels of expenditure on books, etc. Schools would become like private sector firms: seeking to maximize revenue by providing a product that the market wanted, efficiently allocating resources and gaining their own rewards according to the market evaluation of their product.

i   What type of diversity of educational provision might result if a voucher were introduced? In what ways would you like to see schools become different?

ii   The government is concerned over the quality of hygiene in restaurants and hotels — how does it exert influence in this area? In what ways could the government still exercise some control over education under a voucher system?

iii   What are the arguments for and against allowing parents to 'top up' on a voucher — that is, use the voucher at an expensive 'public' school and make up the extra cost from their own pockets?

iv   One of the arguments put forward in favour of a voucher system is that it would

'make teachers more accountable to the general public who pay their wages'.

What difference would a voucher system make to the employment conditions of teachers? Could there be any possible benefits to teachers from working under such conditions?

150

v   If a voucher system is to be introduced, parents have to make choices about the type of education for their children. One fear often voiced by professional educators is that parents do not have the information on which to make such decisions. What do you think?

vi   Can you think of any other areas of local authority provision where the allocative efficiency might be improved by the introduction of a voucher system?

[12]   Why tax 'houses' anyway?

The list below shows the major items of expenditure faced by local authorities:

Libraries
Youth, community services
Education
Magistrates courts
Planning
Highways
Parks
Street lighting
Probation and after-care service
Fire brigade
Trading standards
Waste disposal
Housing
Social services

i   Which of these services are dependent for their demand upon the number of people who live in the authority?

ii   Which of the services are likely to cost the same per house, irrespective of the number of people living there?

One possible way of viewing the reform of local expenditure and income is that it might revolve around two separate themes:
a   the means of taxing housing
b   a means of getting people to pay according to the extent to which they use the local authority services

iii *Some people would not be able to pay according to use —
how could local authorities still derive a payment from these
people?*

Further reading

There are lots of good charts and tables (and articles) in *Public
Money* (available quarterly from the Chartered Institute of
Public Finance and Accountancy, 1 Buckingham Place,
London SW1; the annual subscription rate to schools is
£7.50). *Local Government Finance in a Unitary State* by C.
Foster, R. A. Jackman and M. Perlman (Allen & Unwin,
1980) is certainly the most comprehensive book on local
government finance — but at £27.50 it is perhaps best borrowed from a library.

Appendix 1: Additional material for schools and students at special rates

1 *Economic Progress Report* from the Treasury can be obtained in bulk from Public Relations Division, Central Office of Information, Hercules Road, London SE1 7DU.

2 *Fiscal Studies*, the journal of the Institute for Fiscal Studies, is made available to schools as part of a special rate membership for £15 annually. Write to the Institute for Fiscal Studies, 1/2 Castle Lane, London SW1E 6DR.

3 The Institute of Economic Affairs offers its publications to schoolteachers and students for a £10 annual subscription. Write to the Treasurer, Institute of Economic Affairs, 2 Lord North Street, London, SW1P 3LB.

4 All the banks make excellent material available to schools – Quarterly Reviews in particular are a splendid source of current, informed and highly readable articles. Any local branch manager will respond enthusiastically to a request from teachers or students. The major banks also sponsor the excellent work of the Banking Information Service, which has recently (1983) published a comprehensive 'Guide to Monetary Policy' and is preparing further topics in what will become a most valuable A-level series to complement the superb material they make available for younger pupils. All material from the banks is at present provided in bulk copies free of charge. The Banking Information Service, 10 Lombard Street, London EC3V 9AT.

5 The Economics Association has been responsible for arranging many of these special school offers and additions are made regularly. News of these is always given in the

Association's journal, *Economics*, which also contains excellent articles on new developments in economics and the teaching of the subject. Write to the Economics Association, Temple Lodge, South Street, Ditchling, Sussex BN6 8UQ.

Appendix 2: Recent A-level questions

Chapter 1: monetary policy

What light does UK experience throw on the difficulties that may be encountered in trying to control the money supply?

Oxford, June 1982

How does the government influence the supply of money in the United Kingdom? Explain how monetary policy can be used to reduce the level of aggregate demand.

JMB, June 1980

What is the Public Sector Borrowing Requirement (PSBR)? Explain how PSBR relates to supply of money in the United Kingdom.

London, June 1981

Outline the function of interest rates in the economy. During 1980 many commentators argued that the interest rates fixed by the British government were 'too high'. Discuss the basis for this view and indicate factors which need to be taken into account in fixing interest rates.

JMB, June 1981

Does a rigorous monetary policy make incomes policy unnecessary?

Oxford, June 1982

a What is 'the velocity of circulation of money'?
b What data would you require to calculate its value for the UK?
c What factors might influence the velocity of circulation in the short run?
d What are the implications of such variability for the Quantity Theory of Money?

Cambridge, June 1981

Chapter 2: pay

Given such factors as trade unions and equal pay legislation, are wages determined any longer by economic forces?

Cambridge, June 1981

What is the marginal productivity theory of wages? Assess the validity of the theory in explaining wage levels in the UK economy.

AEB, June 1980

To what extent does economic theory account for differences in the wages earned by different groups of people?

WJEC, June 1981

Discuss the relevance of marginal productivity for the determination of wages in a mixed economy.

London, June 1981

What effects may trade unions in the UK have on the wage rates and employment of:

a workers in different industries?
b workers in various industries?
c male and female workers?

Oxford, June 1981

Chapter 3: unemployment

Analyse the short-term and long-term economic effects of the government paying an amount slightly greater than unemployment benefit to all 16–19 year olds who enter into full-time study of vocational technical subjects.

Oxford, June 1982

Explain why the objective of full employment may be difficult for a government to achieve.

AEB, June 1980

Discuss the significance for the economy of government schemes for the training and retraining of labour.

London, June 1980

Chapter 4: protectionism

Show how, in theory, free trade among nations leads to an increase in economic welfare. What justification, if any, can you find for the policy of selective import controls advocated by some economists in recent years for Britain.

JMB, June 1980

'Do we need to protect jobs?' If so, why?

Cambridge, June 1982

In international trade what benefits can specialization offer a country that protection cannot?

Cambridge, June 1981

'All the arguments in support of tariffs on trade are short term. In the long-run continuing protection cannot be justified economically'. Discuss.

AEB, June 1980

Examine some of the main factors affecting the growth of the UK's international trade in the 1970s.

Scottish Higher, May 1980

Consider the arguments for and against import controls in the UK.

Oxford, June 1982

Chapter 5: Third World debt

Explain what is meant by 'terms of trade'. What might cause these to move in a country's favour? Illustrate your answer by reference to world experience during the last ten years.

London, June 1981

Evaluate the arguments for increasing the scale of aid from the developed countries to developing countries.

London, June 1982

'A deficit on the balance of payments current account has favourable short-run but unfavourable long-run consequences.' Discuss.

AEB, June 1981

What factors determine the rate of growth of an economy? Why do growth rates differ among countries?

Cambridge, June 1982

Why do the incomes of individuals producing primary products tend to be unstable? What may be done to stabilize their income?

Cambridge, June 1982

Describe the chief characteristics of the developing economies. Does the case for aid to these economies rest purely on political expediency or are there significant economic reasons?

JMB, June 1981

Chapter 6: local authority rates

On what basis may a good or service be thought to be better supplied by the public rather than the private sector?

Cambridge, June 1982

Outline and evaluate the economic arguments for subsidizing the price of school meals provided by local authorities.

AEB, June 1981

Examine the case for a major change in the tax base in Britain away from the taxation of earned income and towards taxation of spending.

AEB, June 1981

What do you understand by economic efficiency? What grounds are there for thinking that resource allocation in the UK is economically inefficient?

Cambridge, June 1982

What factors influence house prices in (a) the UK as a whole and (b) particular areas of a large city?

Oxford, Summer 1981

Acknowledgements

The authors and publishers would like to thank the following for permission to reproduce copyright material:

The Controller of Her Majesty's Stationery Office for Figures 1, 12 and 22 and Table 10; the Institute of Economic Affairs for Figures 3 and 4; Oxford University Press for Tables 5 and 6; *Public Money* for Table 11; *World Financial Markets*, published by Morgan Guaranty Trust Company, for Figures 5 and 19 and Table 8.